GW01605979

THE DON LUSHER BOOK

To Diana
For your support and for the hundred and one things you did to make this book finally happen!

The Don Lusher Book

by DON LUSHER

EPL
EGON PUBLISHERS LTD.
Park Drive, Baldock, Herts SG7 6EW

First Published in 1985
by Egon Publishers Ltd.
Park Drive, Baldock, Hertfordshire SG7 6EW

ISBN 0 905858 35 2

Bookjacket picture by courtesy of
Boosey & Hawkes Ltd.

Printed in England by
Streetsprinters
Park Drive, Baldock, Hertfordshire SG7 6EW

Contents

Don Lusher with Nelson Riddle and Naomi, his wife, holding Holly the cat.

Foreword

18th April, 1985

Don Lusher, besides being one of the true gentlemen of the music business, is a consummate craftsman.

He approaches the trombone with the same thoughtful attention to detail I remember in Tommy Dorsey, the same perfect embouchure, breathing apparatus and 'singing' style I was exposed to as a member of the Dorsey Orchestra.

Certainly any information he imparts to the young trombonist will be of incalculable benefit.

Don's book has my unqualified, enthusiastic support!

Nelson Riddle.

(Nelson Riddle died October, 1985)

Photograph: Christine Murray Studio.

Early Days

I don't seem to have any memories before the age of six, when I started to take an interest in the trombone. I remember using a walking-stick and a brass toasting-fork, with an extension, and imagining I was a 'trombone player'. The first real trombone I owned was an old alto trombone bought by my Aunt Nellie for two pounds. I used to sit on the arm of an easy chair at home and pretend I was on the platform at the Peterborough Citadel. I would blow like mad on the old brass trombone not knowing anything about slide positions or what notes I was playing. It must have been a dreadful noise but it felt wonderful to me.

I went to the local primary school at first; then my mother moved me to a small private school because she was very keen that I should eventually go to the grammar school called Deacons School. I'm afraid that I never paid a great deal of attention to my school work, mainly because my mind was always full of music. I loved ball games and running around with boys and girls in gangs.

Ours was a Salvation Army home so there were always instruments around. I went from trombone to cornet to euphonium to drums on to baritone and then back to trombone. My father played cornet, trombone and later baritone in the S.A. band and my mother was the songster-leader. I would pick up her baton and conduct my band of bears and toys and woe betide anyone who did anything wrong in my band.

My mother's father, who was a keen S.A. bandsman, lived with my grandmother in a small house in Providential Place, Peterborough. One of my early memories was listening to my grandfather practice. He would sit on the tiny staircase with his tuba, practising away. He was a good player and the sound enhanced somewhat by the echo of the staircase, made a great impression on me as a youngster. He was always exhorting me to practice; I didn't really need to be told as I loved playing.

One day my mother went off to London; the same evening she returned with a new trombone for me. It was a Brown of Kennington in nickel silver, had a case and blew beautifully. It was my pride and joy. She paid three pounds ten shillings for it. That was a great deal of money to my parents but to me it was worth every penny. Whenever, I drive through Kennington I always wonder where the Brown factory was and remember that thrill of owning a new trombone. Up until then I had used an old trombone in the Learners' Class and the same again when I entered the Young People's Band.

My father suffered from a very bad nervous breakdown caused by hardship in some of the more difficult positions in the Salvation Army. In those days the medical profession didn't have the knowledge that they have now to deal with it. He was so bad that he was not accepted in the army during the first World War. He had to resign from the Salvation Army and became a commercial traveller for a hardware firm.

Quite often my mother would come to the school in the middle of the morning and bring me home where we would find my father crying his eyes out leaning on the mantlepiece. My mother would say, 'Blarm you, Man'. (This was really swearing as far as she was concerned.) We would persuade him to go to work. We would all get on the bus to wherever it was he was due to go to, probably some small town like Spalding a few miles away. Then we would wait for him, while he quite happily went round the shops selling his goods.

Once the journey was over he was quite all right. He was terribly nervous that something would happen to me and would never let me try to swim or even go near water; consequently I didn't learn to swim until I was an adult. I did the Normandy landings during the War with a full pack on, unable to swim! Eileen taught me to swim the first year we were married, when the Squadronaires were in Clacton.

I think that, because of his illness and his consequent nervousness, my father was not much of an influence in my life, but my mother who was a very strong, emotional character, had a very great effect on me. I am very sorry that neither of them lived long enough to see me play with the great brass bands; they would have really been proud of me. I still monitor my behaviour on my mother's standards and I'm afraid there's a great deal I do and have done she would not be happy with!

When I was old enough, I went to Deacon's School. My mother was determined to send me there even though the fees were three guineas a term – a fortune to my parents as my father didn't earn five pounds a week until the end of the War. He was very afraid they would get into debt and would have nothing to do with it, so my mother paid the fees out of the money she made in dressmaking. Often the first day of term would loom terrifyingly close and there was not enough for the fees. 'Don't worry,' she would say, 'the Lord will provide.' And sure enough He did.

I quite liked my time at Deacon's; I think it was a very good and well run school. Unfortunately, I was not very good at my studies and would only work at the subjects I was interested in. I did once come top in geography; that was a great thrill. On the other side of the scale I once got nought in an algebra examination due to being absent with whooping cough. I was so ashamed that I altered the report and put a '4' in front of the '0'. I couldn't take that home to my mother after all her hard work.

The school's headmaster was a Dr Davies; he ran the school with a rod of iron. If for any reason we were sent up before the Head we really did shake in our shoes.

To this day I can remember the staff and, looking back, some of them made a great impression on me. I often

Don Lusher conducting his first 'band'.

Don's parents: Left: his mother, Ethel. Right: Gordon Lusher, his father.

fooled about in the English class and my spelling had to be seen to be believed. One day Mr. F. G. King, the English teacher, suddenly said to me 'Lusher, I'm going to personally take you in hand' – and instead of giving one of the usual punishments like caning, standing in the corner or lines, he picked me up and put me head down in the wastepaper basket.

Several days later, I noticed that he was coming to school on a new racing bicycle. I was fascinated. Eventually, I plucked up courage to ask him about the handle bars. He carefully wrote down the name for me making me help him spell it – 'Loderwasser' – and talked to me about the bike. From that moment on I would do anything for him. Unfortuantely he wasn't able to do much about the spelling but that was my fault – not his. Years later he came to see me in a band contest in Swindon.

We played rugby and hockey in the winter, cross-country running which I hated, and cricket which I love to this day.

We had a tuck shop and, in the break, I would buy a 'Milky Way' which cost a penny. The richer boys would be able to buy a 'Mars' bar at the enormous cost of tuppence. It was at school that I first noticed the different standards of living among the boys. Some always had money for anything they wanted and others, like me, were very restricted. I remember going to some of the richer boys' homes, lovely big houses in pleasant roads, and being taken for rides in their fathers' cars. What a thrill! Very few in our street ever had a car. I had many friends from all walks of life and money never seemed a problem.

We had a school orchestra which wasn't very good. I played drums. Our repertoire was *Minuet in G*, *Cavaleria Rusticana* and suchlike. Looking back on our music lessons, taken by Mr Winterbottom, (nicknamed 'Summer-bum'), they consisted of learning tonic-sol-fa and singing 'Hark, hark the lark' and 'Strawberry Fair'. What a difference from the music lessons of to-day, although he did the best he could with the available equipment.

I go round to various schools giving master-classes and I am struck with the wonderful opportunities the children

Songster leader Ethel Lusher playing the piano at Peterborough Citadel.

Songster leader and Mrs George Briggs, grand parents

of to-day have compared to my school days; especially the wide range of instruments available and the types of music attempted. Sometimes young people write to me asking what grades I obtained and what qualifications I have. I haven't passed any grades nor have I any qualifications, in those days no-one I knew had heard of music examinations. In any case we wouldn't have been able to afford either the music or the examination fees. Playing with the Salvation Army band, listening to music on the radio, my school music lessons and teaching myself are the only training I ever had in my early days.

During my school years, my days with the Salvation Army were getting more and more important to me. I loved the musical side of it and Sunday was my favourite day of the week. Shortly after joining the Senior Band, they had a set of new instruments and I was presented with a S.A. Triumphonic trombone, brand new. I was in heaven for weeks. A short while ago I was looking at the back of one of my old

Peterborough Young People's Band with leader Don Lusher.

Three generations of the Lusher family in the Peterborough Citadel Band. Grandad George, back row second from the left; Father, Gordon, third row, third left; and Don, front row, fifth from left.

tutor books and there it was, advertised at £11 with a gold plated bell.

I listened to bands on the radio and my father took me to all kinds of band concerts. I remember seeing St. Hilda's and Fodens. I was fired with enthusiasm. I began to live from Sunday to Sunday and would sit in the classroom thinking and breathing music. Of course, this had a very bad effect on my school work. I was dying to leave school and work in a shop. Most of all I wanted to play with the Senior Band and play my trombone more and more. The idea of being a professional musician never occured to me; I didn't know anyone who actually earned their living playing an instrument.

When I was just fifteen, my mother had a meeting with Dr Davies who gently suggested to her that, since I was not very academic, (a kind understatement) it was not worth my staying at school and, as I had a job to go to, I could leave. My poor mother had to pay the fees to the end of the school year though; that was the agreement.

That ended my schooling. Now I wish I had learnt more at school. I've regretted it ever since.

Below: Don takes his place in the Peterborough Young People's Band.

Army Days

As time went by I began to feel an attraction for other types of music – symphony orchestras, military bands, some choral works and some types of dance and jazz bands, I remember going to the Embasssy Theatre in Peterborough to see Henry Hall and Joe Loss. I heard Geraldo and Ambrose on the radio, both with fine trombone solos. I bought records of American Bands – Woody Hermann, Harry James, Tommy Dorsey and Dizzy Gillespie.

On leaving school I worked in a large shop, a branch of Selfridges of London. I was doing well and I enjoyed working in various departments but was still thinking about music and wanted to play more and more.

On reaching the age of eighteen, I was called up and went into the Royal Artillery.

I well remember my first night in the Nissen hut with all the other eighteen-year-old intakes, boys from all walks of life from bank clerks to navvies. When I was ready I knelt down by my bed to say my prayers as I had every night of my life. There was a sudden silence; I got up when I had finished and nobody said a word. Gradually the noise and chat started up again. I suppose I was very lucky I could have been really bullied for that.

The next morning on waking I was startled to hear all the coughing and spitting as people reached for the first cigarette of the day. Coming from a Salvation Army family I wasn't used to cigarettes, drink and swearing, all of which was soon to be part of my daily life. I still hate cigarette smoke and excessive drinking.

I tried to get into a band but had to do basic training first. When this was completed I was ready to be posted to a service unit then I really *did* try to get into a band. Eventually the day for my interview came and my formal request was made to a very large Scottish sergeant-major. He looked down at me, shaking his head and saying 'Laddie, we have other plans for ye'. Looking back it was an understandable remark because this was the period of the War when all sorts of important things were happening and my request to go into a band must have seemed very trivial.

I bought a fairly old French trombone and carried it around with me whenever possible even though I wasn't in a band. The Army took me all over the place and I played when I could with Salvation Army bands. By this time preparations were well on the way for the Second Front to open up in Europe. My unit was part of this plan and so we travelled in convoy from Norwich to West Ham Stadium where thousands of us were in a compound waiting to go over for the invasion of Europe. We had to be constantly ready to go and weren't even allowed to undress to sleep; we were simply waiting for the weather to break to go across.

On our second night in the compound, it was announced that we were to have an ENSA concert; Geraldo and His Orchestra, who were appearing at the

Gunner Lusher, No. 1157178, pictured fifth from the left, centre row, in the 34th Signal Training Regiment, Bamber Bridge, 1942.

London Palladium and, in between shows, were to give this concert.

I remember their coach being let into the compound; then they came on to the makeshift stage in front of several thousand troops. Needless to say they were given a great reception. I sat there spellbound in a sort of dream world; it was all wonderful. The lead trombone player was Ted Heath and the sound of his trombone stayed in my mind for a long time. As the show came to a close, I knew that this was what I wanted to do after the War – to be a real professional musician.

After the show was over and they started to get on the coach, I was one of many who tried to get autographs; Maurcie Berman wished me good luck. I never told him about this in later years; now he's dead and I do regret it. I couldn't get near any of the others because they were whisked away quickly to their show at the Palladium. Looking back, I would say, they were Ted Heath, Maurice Berman, Alfie Noakes, Freddy Clayton and Dougie Robinson but in those days, of course, I didn't know them at all.

I went to sleep still with that wonderful sound in my head. Early next morning we went over on the invasion of Europe; you all know the outcome of that.

Looking back, my career in the army was like many others at that time. I was in from 1942 to 1947, was trained to be a signaller in the Royal Artillery and eventually became a driver/operator. That meant driving various types of vehicles and working the radios and communications in them.

When we went over for the invasion of Europe there were times when I was very frightened, I'm certainly no hero. Army life taught me a lot and I don't regret it in any way. I lived with people from all walks of life, mixed with all ranks, learned to rough it and to take care of myself, made a great many friends and most of all, learnt that war is horrible. My trombone playing in the army was negligible, when the war finished we worked our way up through Germany and were stationed at Dortmund. After being there for a short time, I was posted to the 49th Division Concert Party stationed in an old cinema at Arnsberg, Westphalia. We had a band of sixteen under the direction of the pianist Stan Butcher and about ten artists. The whole concert party was under the direction of Hugh Paddock, a captain in those days.

We had shows all over the place. Every now and then the band went off to Hamburg to broadcast on the British Forces Network. We were on the air every day for a week – a thrilling experience for me.

It was on these visits that I met my first musicians who were already pros; people like Jackie Armstrong. Ric Kennedy and his wife Joy Conway, Rusty Hurren, Benny Perrin and others. Some of the people working at the radio station at that time have now become household names; Cliff Michelmore, Robin Boyle, Peter King, Johnny Brandon and John Jacobs, brother to David Jacobs. It was a wonderful time for me and I learned so much from it.

My correct name is Gordon Douglas Lusher. Soon after joining the Concert Party the powers that be could not find find room for 'Gordon Lusher' on a poster, so they compromised by using half of my christian name — just the last three letters — 'Don'. It stuck, and to this day I have been known as Don.

When I joined the band I couldn't even read in bass clef, in brass bands tenor trombones play always in the treble clef. People were helpful and I made the most of my time.

Eventually my rank went up to sergeant and it was from this group that I ended my army days.

Demobbed

After being demobbed from the army in 1947, I went back to Peterborough for a time and had to decide whether to go back to my shop life or to try to become a professional musician. Much against both my parents' wishes, I decided to have a go. Their conception of professional musicians was one of heavy drinking, smoking, loose women, insecurity and late nights. My father above all wanted me to have a steady, secure job.

I used most of my fifty pounds gratuity from the army, to buy an old Conn 24H trombone from the Lew Davis shop in Charing Cross Road. On reflection, from then until now I have played a host of wonderful trombones, the only drawback being that, as good as they are, none of them play themselves; it's all down to the player. Its often said in the profession 'He's so good he could make a piece of gas pipe sound good' – and it's probably true!

I knew no-one connected with the music business in Peterborough, so I joined Stan Butcher, the band leader from my army days, who had gone to live at Pembroke Dock in Wales. He had married a Welsh girl. He formed a small band down there and we took anything that we could get. This proved to be very little. I was staying in digs and using the rest of my gratuity to live on.

Then we got some work in a ballroom in Tenby. To help with our expenses, some of us lived in an old wooden workman's hut by the roadside and took full advantage of the public conveniences nearby. It all went from bad to worse; I knew that I must do something for myself. I spent my time practising, listening to bands on the radio and longing to be part of it all. One day in the *Melody Maker*, I saw that Joe Daniels was advertising for a trombone player. I applied and was given a date for the audition.

I did the audition for Joe Daniels and his Hot Shots and got the job. I was thrilled but alas, after one month the band broke up and I was again out of work. This time for a long time.

I had to go back to Peterborough and my Dad tried to talk me into getting a 'proper job'. One day, out of the blue, I got a telegram to go to the Hammersmith Palais and do an audition for Lou Preager. I did the audition on a Saturday morning, got the job and joined the band right away, doing a live broadcast that same night. The band played six afternoons and nights every week for which I was to be paid eleven pounds. I felt like a millionaire and sent a triumphant telegram to my parents right away. They were delighted for me but still extremely nervous about the type of life I was embarking on.

I had nowhere to live in London so Rusty Hurren and his wife kindly let me stay with them for a time. I had to sleep on the floor but what did that matter? Jackie Armstrong, who was one of my idols, was also staying in the same house and had just joined Ted Heath. Rusty and Jacky were old friends I had met in my army days.

Singer Eileen Orchard with Don pictured on their wedding day.

My stay with Lou Preager at Hammersmith Palais was a good time for me as a musician and also at a personal level. It was an excellent band; Lou was a hard taskmaster and demanded high standards of playing and appearance. We wore lounge suits in the afternoon and dinner suits in the evening. The girl singer had to wear an afternoon dress and a long glamorous dress for the evening show. I well remember Eileen Orchard, the singer with the band, getting into terrible trouble because one afternoon she turned up (looking lovely) in a jumper and skirt. Lou called her up to his room after the show and told her he didn't want any singer of his looking like a housewife!

While at the Palais, I had the opportunity to meet many musicians who used to call in to listen and for a chat. We had many guest bands, including Ted Heath; I would listen avidly, watch and try to learn anything I could.

I was a member of the vocal group from the band called 'The Sunnysiders' and soon fell in love with Eileen Orchard, asking her to marry me. We invited all the band together with Lou for a congratulatory drink between shows on our engagement. However the next day Lou asked to see us both separately. He pointed out that we were both young and that we would damage each others careers if we married. We ignored his advice and were married on March 7th, 1948. As it turns out he was quite correct; Eileen gave up singing very soon after we were married and never returned to it, so in fact her career was ruined. We had two lovely sons, David and Philip; she always helped me in my career and enjoyed the fruits of it so I do hope her sacrifice was worth it and she didn't mind too much. Now we shall never know; she died in 1981.

After a good spell of eighteen months I was offered a job with the famous Maurice Winnick playing at the fabulous Ciro's Club. I was to be paid twenty pounds a week which seemed a fortune; so I left Lou and joined Mr Winnick.

The band was made up of well-known players who did some studio work in the daytime and played this job at night. I have to say that some of them gave me a pretty hard time right from the first rehearsal as I was not known at all to most of them.

In fact, two of the saxophone players never spoke one word to me the whole time I was in the band.

The first afternoon rehearsal I was there, one of the trumpets said to Jock Bain:

'Who's the trombone?'

'Don Lusher,' he replied.

'Where's he come from?'

'Lou Preager', Jock said.

'Good God, a palais band!'

I might very well have had leprosy.

Other members were very helpful, especially Freddy Clayton and Monia Lita. The other trombone was Jock Bain; he was a wonderful player and I learned so much from him.

We played mostly show tunes but very softly and to some very rich people. Sir Malcolm Sargent often came in and would request Jock Bain to play a tune, usually *Stella by Starlight*. Sometimes Royalty would come in.

We had two trumpets and two trombones, so I mostly had to play the third trumpet parts up an octave to sound like a third trumpet. I also sang in the vocal group.

Looking back, I don't think I was happy but, of course, the money was grand and we were expecting our first child, David. After only one month, Mr Winnick called me over and said that I must go. He said there was nothing really wrong with my playing but I had better go out to gain some more experience and become a star; he could really only have stars in his band! I was shattered and that night I walked all the way home from Leicester Square to Earls Court.

Out of work again, but this time it was different. I had responsibilities – a wife, a baby on the way and a flat with a high rent. Whatever would I do?

(To this day, Freddy Clayton says to me when we meet, 'Are you busy, Don?' – and then 'Well, when you're not, I know about a good job at Ciro's!' – and we have a good chuckle.)

Eileen and Don with their two sons, David and Philip.

The Squadronaires

After getting the sack from Maurice Winnick, I had a lucky break by being asked to contact the Squadronaires. This was, of course, a band composed of some of our best musicians. They had volunteered to go into the RAF and had been formed into an official RAF band. It was indeed a wonderful band. After the war was over and they were de-mobbed, they stayed together and were very successful.

The two trombones were George Chisholm and Eric Breeze, the latter a very fine Dorsey-type player. At this time he had decided to leave the band and go into studio work, thus there was a vacancy for a trombone player. In fact, Eric Breeze left the Squads to go into my old job with Maurice Winnick at Ciros and to do studio work during the day. Eric and Maurice had been friends for some time. Still it's an ill wind that blows nobody any good!

I made the phone call and was told to do an audition whilst the Squadronaires were doing a rehearsal for a broadcast at the old Cripplegate BBC Studios. I was nervous; the pieces I had to play were pretty tough. However I did my best and they told me I could have a month's trial on either side. I was very pleased and relieved in view of my commitments.

The band did one-night stands, some weeks in theatres, broadcasts and recordings. My trombone book was hard because Eric was such a fine player and I had a lot of his solos to play. But in addition to the solos, George Chilsholm had written arrangements which involved he and Eric playing unison choruses which were mostly very fast and hard. Much of the book was also written in treble clef concert and, in those days, I was fairly slow at reading in that pitch. I just got stuck in and did a lot of work on the pieces at home. There was a great deal of help from George; he was wonderful to sit by and listen to. Tommy McQuater was like a father to me; others like Jimmy Watson, Cliff Townsend, Jimmy Durrant, Andy McDevit, Ronnie Aldridge, Jock Cummings and Jimmy Miller were all very helpful.

When the month's trial was over, no one said anything. Finally on the last evening of the month, I timidly asked Tommy McQuater if there was any news. He smiled and said 'Has anyone said anything?' I said, 'No.' He smiled again and said, 'Well, I should stay if I were you'.

Later that week, Arthur Maiden the bass player and manager, rang me at home. We didn't have a phone in our basement flat at Lexham Gardens, Earls Court, but had to use the call box in the hall. He said it was decided that I should stay with the band; he was offering £17.50 a week for four dates – anything over that was to be paid pro-rata. I agreed to that and rushed down to tell Eileen; also to ask her what 'pro rata' meant. I had no idea. The Squads were a co-operative band. I was the first non-original member, so was paid only a salary. This was adequate when we were not touring but I well remember being broke when we were touring and staying at places like The Grand Hotel, Manchester, with the rest of the band. They were all on very good money; which was fine as they were all good and experienced musicians. Yet I was horrified at seeing some of them gambling and using their wage-packets as stakes!

When I was with the Squads, we used to play at Green's Playhouse in Glasgow for a month at a time. We played each day, afternoons and evenings, with only Sunday off. That left only the mornings free. Andy McDevitt, a marvellous clarinet player, impressed on me the importance of daily practice. Very often we would play some studies together. Andy was one of the many people I really admired. I've always thought it good to mix with people who are better than I am – and not just in music – hoping some of their greatness will brush off on me!

After finishing the afternoon session I would go back to the digs in Hill Street, have some tea, sit in front of the gas fire and study chords and progressions. I remember writing them out from C major through to C thirteenth and so forth and so on. Every little piece of musical education was painstakingly achieved by hard work and sometimes almost by accident.

The Squadronaires, in relaxed mood, at Butlins holiday camp Clacton with Don Lusher and George Chisholm on Trombone.

For the past few years, I have been giving teach-ins and Master Classes all over the world. I always do this with a great sense of responsibility and would hate to give any player wrong information or lead them along the wrong track. Not having had a formal musical education myself, I have to be very careful when teaching young players. All I have to offer is my experience. I have worked with some of the greatest musicians in the world; much of their expertise has brushed off on me which in turn, I am able to pass on to others.

It is much more difficult today for young players to get the experience they need. Where are the big bands touring the country, the clubs full of musicians? Very few and far between. My generation were lucky to have that experience; unlucky in that few of us had the opportunity to formally learn the basics of our profession.

Only a short time ago, I was asked to give a Master Class on brass playing at the Royal College of Music in London. It was going well; besides the students there were a number of professors in the audience. They had come in to listen, I knew them well – each one an expert player. As I was speaking, there was a sudden thought: *'What am I doing here?'*

Members of the Jack Parnell Orchestra. From left to right, Jim Wilson, Harry Roache, Jack Parnell, Jimmy Watson and Don Lusher.

At that very moment, one of the students decided to ask me what I thought about music grades and colleges. There was a moment's silence; I grinned and had to come clean and admit my lack of formal education, of how I always felt inferior when being inside a place like the Royal College. How much I would love to go to one of those colleges even today and receive the tuition they all take for granted both in playing and theory. I told them to make the most of it; they have wonderful opportunity. I'm not jealous of them – well not much.

After about three years I wanted to stay at home more so left the Squads and joined Jack Parnell's new band. He had just left Ted Heath. We went into a show featuring Pat Kirkwood and Tommy Trinder at the *Prince of Wales* Theatre. I was on third trombone; the others were Harry Roche and Jimmy Wilson. Again the band was a good one with such players as Ronnie Scott, Bob Burns, Jimmy Watson, Phil Seaman, Sammy Stokes and Max Harris.

It was a good experience; after about a year the show came to an end. Jack re-formed the band and went on the road. I didn't go because I'd been offered a job with Geraldo's Orchestra which appealed to me a great deal.

The Geraldo band was beautiful and real class. Here again you were only paid for what you did; sometimes the band was busy, sometimes not – but we did a lot of broadcasting. The band was made up of outstanding musicians who, besides working for Gerry, did a lot of studio work.

I went in as fourth trombone, again to be led by Jock Bain alongside Maurice Pratt and Jack Thirwell. Things were shared out so well we all had leads and solos to play. It was a fine section; Jock could be tough if things were not right. It was a joy to work with such fine musicains as Derek Abbott, Alan Franks, Albert Hall, Jiver Hutchinson, Dougie Robinson, Keith Bird, Phil Goody, Eric Delaney, Ivor Mairants, Jack Collier and Sid Bright. The vocal department was also very strong: Jill Day, Eve

Boswell, Bob Dale and Derek Francis. We played some of the best arrangements I have ever played. I was very happy in the band and now my studio work was building up well. I was doing work for Lad Busby, Harry Roche and Jock Bain – they were the big three in those days.

About this time, Jackie Armstrong left Ted Heath. From time to time Albert Hall and I did sessions with Ted's band to make the brass up to ten. Ted called me one day and said that he would like me to join the band. He made me a very good offer but I was happy as I was and so I said, 'Thank you but no'. I still did odd dates with the band and from time to time he asked me to join and still I declined. Then one day he called me to his office, laid out the full situation and made me a final offer. He gave me a week to make up my mind and told me he had made a similar offer to another very well-known player who wanted to join. This really made me think. I met Jock Bain and asked in confidence for his advice. He told me that it was a wonderful opportunity and I should take it. I gave in my notice to Gerry who was not pleased and didn't speak to me for two weeks, although afterwards we remained good friends. I did my last date with Gerry one morning (a BBC broadcast), had lunch and joined Ted's band for a teatime broadcast.

Enough has been said about the Heath band already but I do feel that I would like to put down on paper some of my own memories and feelings about that band.

Ted Heath

Whilst still in the Army and stationed in Germany, I already knew of the Heath band's wonderful reputation from articles and hearing them in BBC broadcasts. I made up my mind that I must try to see them in the flesh during my next leave in the UK. They were appearing at Hammersmith Palais on the last night of my leave so I arranged for one of my army friends to come with me to see them. We decided to leave the show early in order that we would have time to catch the boat train to Harwich.

The band was due on at eight-thirty; a little before seven we were outside the Palais in a queue which stretched well past the fire station. Within the hour we were near the bandstand around which was a barricade. Even at that time it was five or six fans deep.

There in front of us were the empty music stands with the famous *TH* on them; Jack Parnell came on to the stand to adjust his drumkit, everything he did was watched avidly by the fans. As we were going into the building I remember seeing Kenny Baker and Les Gilbert, both clad in beautiful Crombie overcoats, arriving to do the show. As time went on the crowd became larger and larger with the atmosphere increasingly electric. Just before eight-thirty the lights dimmed and suddenly there was the voice of Paul Carpenter announcing 'Sixty minutes right off the top with Ted Heath and his Music.' There in a blaze of light was this wonderful group of musicians, beautifully turned out. And what a sound! It was a revelation for me to see and hear them at such close quarters.

It was all breathtaking; the reaction of the crowd was tremendous. Without going into details I can tell you that it was all so good that we didn't leave early enough to catch the boat-train. We were, therefore, late back from leave and were charged, receiving a week confined to barracks with a pay stoppage as well. It wasn't a big price to pay for such a wonderful evening. Little did I know that one day I would also be a member of that band appearing on that same bandstand many, many times!

Ted himself was very strict. He paid very well and the conditions were good. He loved a good laugh and, if you wanted it, he could talk to you like a father. Above all he was a fanatic about his band; he thought about it all the time. He set a perfect example and hated people being off sick. 'Death is the only excuse,' he would say. He was a clever man, a fine trombone player and a good business man with a lot of know-how knowing what to play and who to have in the band. He was very good to me. I shall always owe him so much and I learned a great deal during my nine-and-a-half years with his band.

The singers were each very strong characters in their own right, yet good to work with. Dickie Valentine, Lita Roza and Denis Lotis are all household names. The chief thing about the band was its team spirit; it was a unit you were proud to belong to. We had a great deal of fun although there could be the occasional domestic argument in a dressing room. But once we were on the stand we just got stuck in to our work. We had to work very hard; Ted demanded it.

Our families enjoyed being part of the band too. Every summer we went to Blackpool for one month and Torquay for two weeks; our wives and children joined us for all or part of that time. I have memories of all the kids playing cricket on the beach and of watching them grow up year by year. My sons remember those times; we often talk of them with pleasure.

Ted was always very strict about the band's dress which had to be clean, neat and correct. We had several uniforms and sometimes changed in the interval. Imagine what that would cost today!

One night, we were all in the dressing room getting ready when Ronnie Verrell noticed that he had forgotten to pack his black socks. He tried to borrow a pair, but no-one had anything suitable. This was desperate; his position in the band was on a fairly high rostrum right in the centre of the set-up, almost impossible for Ted not to notice. So he did the only thing possible. He went to work with the black shoe-polish brushing it well, into his feet, ankles and about ten inches up the leg. On with his shoes and he was ready. The concert went well; Verrell played like an angel and Ted made no comment. We can assume that for once Ted's eagle eyes missed it. Poor old Ron! It took him ages to get the stuff off; I dread to think what the sheets were like that night.

Ted was very unsympathetic regarding illness and hated anyone to be off work. He set a proper example by being on the stand when quite unwell. While we were on tour in the USA, we played Cincinnati on a Sunday with shows afternoon and evening. Ted was quite ill. He would announce an item, start the band, walk casually off to the wings to vomit into a waiting bucket and walk back with a smile. Another announcement, start the band and off into the wings. This went on throughout

Ted Heath with his star-studded band. Front row, left to right; George Hunter, Roy Willox, Leslie Gilbert, Danny Moss, Henry Mackenzie, Denis Lotis, Lita Roza, Dickie Valentine, Ric Kennedy, Wally Smith, Don Lusher, Jimmy Coombes. Back row; Frank Horrocks, Johnny Hawkesworth, Ronnie Verrall, Duncan Campbell, Bobby Pratt, Stan Reynolds and Ronnie Hughes.

the show. Between shows and during the interval he lay down in his dressing-room. This went on for several days. He was a real trouper himself and naturally had little patience with anyone who fussed.

Another thing he couldn't stand was bad time-keeping, expecting everyone to be on time for everything. We all knew that if we were late there would be trouble.

One Sunday afternoon the band was rehearsing for a Palladium concert. The call for the rehearsal was two-thirty; everyone was there except one of the trombone players. (Not me!) Time went on and he still didn't appear, the atmosphere becoming increasingly tense. Eventually, the absentee made his entrance.

Ted scowled at him: 'Well?' The poor trombone player looking very sickly explained that he had knocked a man over and killed him. Ted just said 'Oh, O.K., then lets get on.' The explanation is not to be taken too seriously and it certainly wasn't true. But is gives you an insight into how Ted ran the band and how important is was to him.

Ted Heath could be very generous with his time if you had a problem. From time to time he was like a father to me and to the other members of the band. He hated to sack anyone and it gave him a great deal of heartache.

Still it was quite possible to get the sack from the band usually to make way for another player who Ted thought would be better for the band. I suppose that is one reason why the band stayed at the top for so long. The band right from the start was full of wonderful players; let me mention some of them who thrilled me during my stay:

Bobby Pratt (trumpet)
Eddie Blair (trumpet)
Ronnie Hughes (trumpet)
Duncan Campbell (trumpet)
Wally Smith (trombone)
Keith Christie (trombone)
Johnny Edwards (trombone)
Les Gilbert (alto saxophone)
Roy Willox (alto saxophone)

Members of the Ted Heath Band at the Conn Instrument factory, Elkhart, USA in 1956.

Ronnie Chamberlain (alto saxophone)
Bob Efford (tenor saxophone)
Red Price (tenor saxophone)
Don Rendall (tenor saxophone)
Ronnie Verrall (drums)
John Hawkesworth (bass)
Frank Horrocks (piano)
Stan Tracey (piano)

There were others long before I joined and also afterwards not forgetting the band managers, all who did well after leaving Ted. Let me mention two whilst I was there: Colin Hogg and Wally Palmer, both great people, and two others before my time, Derek Bolton and Harry Walters.

The first week I joined the band we were top of the bill at the Finsbury Park Empire for the week, we did a Sunday concert at the Palladium, a Decca recording session, a Luxembourg broadcast and a BBC broadcast. It wasn't always like that but we were a busy band. It had to be to support Ted and his family, the band and singers, plus a manager and the full office staff.

Besides the sessions and one-night stands that we did, other highlights were the tour of Australia and New Zealand in 1955, completed in a month, our tours of the USA from 1956 onwards, Sunday Palladium concerts and appearing at Royal Command performances. Most musicians in the band business aimed one day to be in the Heath Band; I shall be forever grateful that I was lucky to pass through its ranks.

In 1956, Ted Heath and His Music went to the USA for the first time. We had five days going over in the Queen Mary, a wonderful experience in itself. By the time we reached New York excitement was very high; we knew there would be so much to see and hear, so many people to meet, besides our own activities with the band. We were also nervous about the American reaction to the band; they had so many good bands of their own. Once in the hotel, we went through the papers to see what was on. Playing at the Statler Hotel was the Dorsey Brothers Orchestra. for many of us this was first choice.

Before long, a large group of us found ourselves at this very fine hotel, quickly finding the room in which the band was playing. It was a beautiful room and certainly not cheap. We spoke to some waiters and asked if it were possible for us to come in for a time and listen to the band. They called over the Head Waiter; after telling him that we were part of the Ted Heath band from the UK, he took us in. We sat at a large table and they brought us drinks. They couldn't have been more kind. There before us was the full Dorsey sound. Tommy was playing *I'll never smile again;* it brought a lump to my throat. The band looked marvellous and sounded wonderful. What can I say about Tommy? It's all been said before!

He played a lot of solos. There was a very fine trombone section with no bass trombone – it wasn't in fashion in those days. He conducted and did the announcing. At times he would play full and loud; at other times in a whisper. From time to time, brother Jimmy Dorsey would come on the stand to play solos and to join the section making six saxes. When they had their break Tommy and Jimmy brought the band over to meet us; Ted introduced us one by one. What a thrill it was! Everyone was very kind and we had a wonderful time.

Some of us went for four evenings; we spent time in their band room — which incidentally was beautifully laid out — made friends with many of the musicians including Louis Belson and Charley Shavers, and saw the band in a live broadcast. I also was able to handle and play Tommy's trombone. It was a King 2B, gold plated.

One night after the band had finished work, Tommy came over to me and we had a real man-to-man talk. He told me of his plans for the band. A big man, very tall with short white hair, he seemd so full of life. Indeed both brothers did. Within a fairly short time both Tommy and Jimmy were dead; it seemed unbelievable. What a tragic loss to so many people.

The first concert of our US tour was at the Carnegie Hall. We rehearsed for two days and did the show on the third day. The thought of playing at the Carnegie Hall was a daunting one. It is a beautiful and famous place; as we went in for rehearsal we remarked to each other about the many well-known artists who had performed on that stage.

As the time for the show came nearer, so the atmosphere became more and more tense. Every member of the band was on edge. The 'Four Freshmen' were on the show with us; even they were nervous. We knew that a lot of famous band-leaders and musicians were going to be in the audience; this

Ted's trombone section playing their new Conn Trombones. Left to right: Keith Christie, Wally Smith, Don Lusher and Jimmy Coombes.

made us even more jittery. Jerry Mulligan and Errol Garner came into our bandroom to give encouragement.

Eventually we found ourselves on stage playing to a packed house. After the signature tune and *Kings Cross Climax* we just got stuck in and gave our best. Everyone played very well; you really could feel the team spirit within the band. Almost everyone had solos to play all of which went down well. The audience seemed to be most enthusiastic. At the end of the show Ted and the band had to take many calls. Ted stood in front of the band taking all those calls with tears in his eyes. One of his dreams had come true. He had taken a British Band to the USA – in fact to the home of big bands — and the band had triumphed. There was a glow among the band after the concert as we chatted to people who had been in the audience. Some were famous musicians, some were fans, others had just come to the concert out of curiosity to see and hear this British Band.

We stayed up late and in the early hours of the morning, bought the morning papers on Broadway. All was well, the reviews were fine, we had done a good job and everyone was thrilled. Decca issued an album of the live concert. It's a good moment to look back on.

Nat King Cole

One morning in the summer of 1984, Diana (my second wife) answered a telephone call from an old colleague of hers, Norma Corney. Diana had worked at the ATV studios, Elstree at the same time as Norma when they were both Production Assistants. After they had had a chat about old times, Norma explained that she hadn't really telephoned Diana but wanted to talk to me. She didn't know we had married and was quite surprised when Diana answered the phone.

Norma was working for an American film producer, Ernest Tidyman, who was creator of the black detective, *Shaft*. He had also written the film-script for the drugs drama, *The French Connection*. He was in London doing research for his next project, a film about Nat King Cole, and he wanted me to tell him the details of the night the Heath Band played in Birmingham, Alabama with the singer.

The incident was as clear in my mind as if it were yesterday; that is until they started asking questions in detail. For example, was it the first or second house? Were you playing in front of the tabs or behind them, and so on. It really is amazing how little of the details one can remember after nearly thirty years.

In was in 1956, during the same tour with the Heath Band that we met the Dorsey Brothers. The show was a package with Nat King Cole, June Christie, The Four Freshmen and the Ted Heath Band. It was a great experience for us to be part of such a package. The tour was very hard at times from a travelling point of view but a wonderful opportunity for us to see the States. Eventually we got down to the Southern States and to Alabama, where we played in a large concert hall in Birmingham. In those days, black musicians were not allowed on the same stage as white musicians, in fact in some towns in the South, we did two concerts each night, one for a black audience and one for white. But for this particular concert none of us can remember whether it was an all white audience, all black or mixed.

It was arranged that Ted's band would play behind a netting so that we couldn't be seen. This was very impractical from a playing point of view and anyway Ted would not hear of it. So, as a compromise, the screen was raised to about head height; we could therefore be seen and heard by the audience.

The first part of the concert was over and now it was Nat's turn to go on. At the front of the stage was Nat; just behind him his coloured group led by Lee Young, brother of Lester Young — fine musicians, lovely people. We were well into the tour by this time and had come to know the group very well. Our band sat behind the group in full view of the audience.

While Nat was singing we suddenly noticed two white men walking down the centre aisle towards the stage. Suddenly they rushed up to him and it seemed that one of them pushed and punched him while the other pulled his legs from under him and he fell backwards over the piano stool. Pandemonium broke out; the audience was on its feet, the police, armed of course, were suddenly on the scene and the concert came to an abrupt end.

Nat was whisked off by the police and we didn't see him again for several days. He was in great danger and the police obviously thought he was safer with them than anywhere else.

Nat's musicians and our band came off the stage and were held under police protection in a back room. We could hear a great deal of shouting and general noise going on outside but, of course, we didn't really know what was going on. What could we say to Nat's musicians? We were all shocked and felt physically sick.

We were kept in that room until the early hours of the morning; then we were taken back by coach to the hotel. We were only given time to pack and then left by coach to go on to the next stop of the tour. Ted was not in the concert hall when all this happened; he had left and gone back to the hotel after the first half and the first he knew of the incident was when it was given out on a television newscast. It wasn't very long before it was in the news in the UK.

We found out afterwards that the police had discovered a car full of guns and ammunition in the concert hall car-park. Apparently the whole incident had been organised by the Ku Klux Klan and could obviously have been very much worse had the police not intervened so promptly.

Nat King Cole missed a few shows but was soon back with us, singing as well as ever. After that night, we felt very uncomfortable for some time but it was good to get on with the show again. As they say, the show did go on!

On the 15th July, 1984, Ernest Tidyman died suddenly in London before I could arrange to meet and tell him all I could remember of the Alabama incident. However, some days later I went up to town to see his widow and talk to her. She is a very brave lady and was determined at that time to go on with her husband's project. I don't know whether or not the film was produced; I shall be very interested to see it if ever it reaches the U.K.

Ted Heath Today

From time to time over the last few years, the Ted Heath Band has been reassembled to give about six concerts a year. The name of the band of course is still owned by Mrs Moira Heath and the family so that nothing can be done without their permission. Some years ago, several people started to take bands out on the road with the Ted Heath name but Mrs Heath soon put a stop to that!

Thames Television decided to do a television show about Ted Heath and His Music and Moira asked me to front the band for this occasion. The show was very well produced by David Clark. Now most of the contacts for concerts come to me and I work with Moira and her daughter, Val Heath. I have the old Heath library stored in my home; in fact, cupboards were built for it in my office because there is so much of it. I also have the original music stands which we use for shows.

Most of the players are chosen from people who were members of the Heath Band at one time or another. I book and pay them myself. Those who have done most of the dates are:

Trumpets: Kenny Baker, Derek Healey, Ronnie Hughes, Duncan Campbell.
Trombones: Wally Smith, Johnny Edwards, Ric Kennedy, Bill Geldard.
Saxophones: Ronnie Chamberlain, Roy Willox, Tommy Whittle, Henry Mackenzie, Eddie Mordue.
Drums: Jack Parnell.
Bass: Lennie Bush.
Piano: Norman Stenfalt.
Singers: Lita Roza, Denis Lotis.

. . . with me playing and fronting the band.

As you can see, it's a star-studded group of musicians. Most of them work in the studios and therefore they are hard to get hold of. They are very well paid for the Heath concerts but if the concerts clash with a television series then it's quite possible to lose quite a few of the people you've already booked! Television pays better than the concerts and no one wants to lose a series for one concert. Freelance musicians must look after their regular work.

The band now works mainly in the London area, excepting one good date in the Spinney Hill Hall for the Northampton Council. We've done this date for about five consecutive years. I get many requests for the band to go out of town to the larger provincial cities; players no longer wish to travel. Their thoughts are that they did all that thirty years ago and they don't want to do it now. They would possibly lose some work because of the time spent travelling but money is not everything and they would have such a great time and the reception of the band would be so wonderful that it would be well worth the effort. I, myself, do quite a lot of travelling making solo appearances and I have a very good time. However it's up to them; I feel they're losing out.

Among the dates we do have been three for the National Westminster Bank; they have been organised by their Head of Public Affairs, Geoff

Burdett who has done a grand job. What a live wire he is. He is still a fan of the band and seems to remember more about us, present and past, than most.

The National Westminster Bank has looked after us handsomely and at the same time raised a great deal of money for charity. They always invite the wives and girl-friends of the band to the concert and to a buffet supper afterwards. This makes the concert like a family re-union for us; we really enjoy it. The atmosphere at the concert is magical every time.

These are the dates we have fulfilled for the National Westminster Bank, all at the Barbican Hall, London:

1982, 11th December with Ray Ellington and his Quartet in aid of Kidney Research.

1983, 18th June with The Ronnie Scott Quintet in aid of Leukaemia Research.

1984, 14th April with George Chisholm and the Jazz Gang in aid of the Mental Health Foundation. This was an anniversary concert 40 years of the Ted Heath Band. The band was founded in 1944.

The first concert on 11th December 1982 was especially pleasing to me because Geoff Burdett asked me to name the charity I would like and if the bank agreed we could do it for that. My wife, Eileen, died in March 1981 of kidney failure due to diabetes and I promised the staff at Dulwich Hospital where she died that I would do something for the renal unit when I could. The 11th December was Eileen's birthday and we raised £15,000 for Kidney Research, part of which was donated to the Dulwich Hospital renal unit. Needless to say, that concert meant a great deal to me.

There is a great deal of organisation for each concert; here's how we go about it. As soon as a concert date is requested and I think most of the band will be able to do it, I get permission from the Heath family, then I book the musicians and singers – eighteen phone calls in all! That's if I'm lucky enough to get everyone on the first call. Then, as the time gets nearer to the concert date, some of the players will have telephoned asking to be released because something else more lucrative has been offered. This is really the biggest headache of the entire organisation.

Then I go through the library; I like to change the programmes and play some music from all the different periods of the band's history. This can be difficult because some of the music is so old you can hardly read it, some parts or pages of parts are missing and, worse still, some of the scores are lost. All the music reeks of cigarette smoke and when the cupboard doors are opened it really hits you.

When I am selecting a programme, I bear in mind a shape and try to build a climax at the end of each half. I try to keep each half to a maximum of one hour; any longer and an audience gets tired. I then have to sort out the music, putting each part in order and into the individual's pad of music. After that, salary cheques are made out. The running order of the programme has to be typed and photocopied, one for each player and singer and several for the stage staff at the venue. Diana often helps me with all this detailed work.

On the day of the show, I go to the concert hall and set out the stand with the band manager. We usually arrive about an hour before any of the musicians so that we can iron out any snags. For the last year or so John Miller, Glen Miller's nephew, has been our band manager and a very fine one he is too; he really understands big bands. He sings with the Miller band run by Glen Miller's brother, Herb Miller, so we can't always get him.

We have a three-hour rehearsal with a fifteen-minute tea break half way through. I rehearse the band first, then the singers, finishing with the small groups. I have to push the band all the time because of the time factor; even so, we have interuptions because of a multitude of minor irritations – bad seating, draughts, lighting, can't hear the bass, drums too loud, dressing rooms too small and one-hundred-and-one other tiny troubles. However, somehow we get through it all.

I like the band to have about one and a half hours off before the concert so that they can relax, eat and get changed comfortably. I go to my room to go over the announcements which have already been prepared and rehearsed to myself while driving to the concert. Ted always kept an old envelope in the car; if he thought of anything for the concert, or something that he didn't want to forget, he would jot it down there and then. It really impressed me at the time because it showed that he was always thinking about the band and didn't stop scheming and planning even when he was driving. I check on my solos and see that the complimentary tickets are all at the stage door, properly marked, and that the guests are greeted and shown to their seats. Diana is a great help with all this. A quick bite to eat, maybe a rest, visit the stage and see that everything is tidy; then a wash and change. Then is the moment when I wonder if everything will work out all right!

Time to go; we always try to start dead on time just as Ted did. The stage manager gives me the cue to start; we play the signature tune *Listen to My Music* which never ceases to thrill me. From then on we all get stuck in and do our job. What a thrill it is to stand out in front and listen to that sound. It's always very good but sometimes they play like angels. I don't try to copy Ted in any way; I think that would be silly. But I do bear in mind all the time what he would have wanted – his likes and dislikes.

In the interval, I go to my room and think about the second half, maybe meet people as well. In a second half I aim to build the programme to a climax so that the audience will leave wanting more. The reception and the applause at the end is a great thrill but most of the satisfaction, for me at any rate, comes from doing the complete package including the organisation and the rehearsal.

Whilst giving a Ted Heath concert at the Fairfield Hall, Croydon in 1976, we were nearly at the end where I was thanking everyone concerned, when I was aware of some activity at the side of the stage. As I looked round I saw Moira Heath walking towards me carrying a trombone. I couldn't imagine what was going on but was soon to find out. In front of a packed house and with all those wonderful musicians behind me, she presented me with Ted's old trombone, inscribed on the bell: *Presented to Don Lusher on the 9th November 1976 Ted Heath's trombone with thanks for perpetuating his memory.* Moira made a moving speech; I was speechless and caught completely off guard.

It is a great honour to have the trombone and I shall treasure it for the rest of my life. It hangs on the wall of my office creating great interest to my many visitors from all over the world. While I was with the band he played on

A moving moment as Mrs. Moira Heath presents Don Lusher with Ted Heath's trombone at the Fairfield Hall, Croydon in 1976.

The Ted Heath Band of today at the Barbican, London.

this trombone – a silver bell King 2B – together with an Olds.

After the curtain comes down, all that is left is to supervise the packing up, thank everyone, meet people including the Heath family and see what everyone thought. Then I drive home and think about what it was really like – was it as good as it felt? – how can we improve it next time? – and so on. As I go to sleep I'm always tired and generally happy. But having been a band leader for a day, the next morning I'm back to being a trombone player working for someone else!

Elstree

In 1961, I left the Ted Heath band. I had had enough of touring and could see that it would be better for my future if I became my own boss and worked mostly in the studios as a free--lance musician. One of my main connections was with Jack Parnell's ATV Band.

We were based at the Wood Green Studios, doing shows like 'Saturday Night Spectacular', and 'Sunday Night at the London Palladium'. Later, in 1962, ATV moved to Elstree and to an impressive complex of studios once used for making films. They were set in pleasant gardens with ample car parking space. There was an excellent canteen and an attractive bar which made working very comfortable.

We were a full-size band with a string section and backing singers, usually The Mike Sammes Singers. The arrangers were some of the best in the business; so were the musicians many of whom were ex-Ted Heath members. With me in the trombones were Lad Busby and Jack Armstrong; then either Chris Smith, Johnny Marshall or Jim Wilson. We played for many types of television shows including Morecambe and Wise.

It was at Elstree that I first saw my second wife, Diana. She was Rita Gillespie's Production Assistant. Rita and Diana had just completed a pop show with Jack Good called *Oh, Boy!* for ABC television. We worked on several shows together, one was called *All, That Jazz.* Diana was married at that time to drummer Bobby Kevin. I never imagined that one day she would become my wife. She always looked so efficient with her clipboard that she frightened me to death! The only conversation we ever had was me saying 'Hello, Diana. How's Bob? Is he busy?' and her reply, 'Yes, fine'. Everytime we met we said the same thing. Hardly the start of something big!

We also did many 'specials' for the USA; one with Barbara Striesand won an award. The long-running Tom Jones and Englebert Humperdinck series also involved us. For about five years I was in a smaller unit of about twelve players who did the music each week for *The Muppets.* It was a talented team to work with; we had some great guest artistes on the shows; Dizzie Gillespie and Buddy Rich to name but two.

Around 1983, Elstree was closed and Jack's band ended. What a shame that was for everyone, technicians, production staff and artists and musicians alike. Everyone was so sad that a special video was made up of all the highlights of the Elstree productions, just for people who worked there – not for transmission – so that we could all have something to look back on. Many of the Elstree staff are now based at the Central Studios in Nottingham so I still see them when I go up there.

The closing of Elstree ended a very happy and interesting period of my life.

Frank Sinatra

It has been my privilege on many occasions to be a member of the orchestra chosen to accompany Frank Sinatra. The members are London-based studio musicians and we have done various tours not only in the UK but in Europe and the Near East.

One of the great joys is just playing the music, written by some of the best arrangers in the world. The atmosphere at these concerts is quite fantastic, very exciting and very moving. It's a great pleasure for us to see such vast crowds of people go away so full of the joyful experience.

The conductors on these Frank Sinatra tours have been Billy Miller, Don Costa or Vince Falcone Jr. He also takes his own four-piece rhythm section of really great players. The trombone section usually sits beside this section; take it from me it's quite something!

A little about the man himself. I have found that, providing everything is right, he is fine to work with; if that is not the case, he will let you know about it and get it put right immediately.

With his early background of singing with bands, he understands musicians. On one occasion when there was a long break between shows at the Royal Albert Hall, we had a get-together with him during which I talked about Tommy Dorsey. He told me many interesting things about Tommy and other band-leaders of that time.

I've found it absorbing to study his know-how with an audience. He tends to move around the orchestra during a concert so sometimes he is just a yard or so away from you. His communication with the audience, his mannerisms, his announcements, the way he walks on and off are simply fascinating. If there is a solo to play he will move close and those blue eyes will go right through you. Whenever I have a solo I choose not to look at him!

Mostly we have two, three or four rehearsals without him. By the end of the second one the playing will be perfect; on the next rehearsal Frank will be there. He takes over completely! He'll stop and start the orchestra and bring it all to life. I don't say this in any way against his musical directors. They all do a great job. I just have to try and point out the special know-how and personality of the man! He's a stickler for tempos, dynamics, feel, intonation and the emotions of his music. I'm sure I don't need to speak about his singing but I must say that you can always hear the words and in each song he tells a story.

From September 17th to 22nd 1984, I played for Frank at the Royal Albert Hall as part of a fine band made up of British free-lance musicians. Buddy Rich and His Band opened the show and played for the first thirty minutes; there was an interval and we went on for Frank's spot – exactly one hour.

Every night before going on, we listened to Buddy's young and exciting American musicians; the oldest was twenty-seven! The Hall was packed for every one of the six shows and, in spite of an extremely bad press, each performance went down well and there was a wonderful gala atmosphere. The printed programmes were works of art, each one like an LP sleeve, and inside the cover a circular programme, like a record, with the title *Sinatra for the Record.*

Inside the round programme were many excellent photographs of Frank and other famous people he has worked with, lists of his records and other features. Benny Green had written a very fine account of Frank's career entitled *Thanks for the Melody*. I found it interesting, especially the stories relating to how some of the songs came to be recorded. The programme also listed the musicians in Frank's group with a short life-story for each of them including Joe Parnell (who was musical director on this session), Tony Mottola, Irv Cottler and Don Baldwin. All of them are excellent musicians; they have been associated with Frank for many years, Irv Cottler for twenty-five.

Irv Cottler admired my Marks and Spencer evening dress suit so much that he asked me to get him one and send it to him in the States. I wonder if the people at Marks know their dress suit is on stage with Frank Sinatra!

From our point of view it was a great week of playing beautiful music with a good band and seeing and hearing once again this beautiful artist at work. On the night that Diana came to see the show, Frank sang a lovely song

Frank Sinatra recording in London with Robert Farnon and trombonists Wally Smith and Don Lusher. (Photograph: Dezo Hoffmann Ltd).

Don Lusher soloing with Frank Sinatra. Bass Trombonist is Ray Premru.

called *Thanks to the Band* which is a tribute to all the bands he's ever played with. One of the lines is particularly apt; I don't know the exact words but he thanks all the musicians, some of them well-known and some of them unknown. He is definitely a 'band singer'.

After the Albert Hall, three horn players, one percussionist and I augmented Buddy's band to play for Frank in Paris and Vienna. It turned out to be a marvellous experience in more ways than one. We stayed at the Hotel George V in Paris, one of the best hotels I have ever been in with many lovely little touches, like chocolates in the room and every kind of toiletry you can imagine in the bathroom. The Buddy Rich band were goggle-eyed. Many of them had never been to Europe before and the whole trip was a thrill.

In Paris and Vienna, Buddy played his four numbers, then Frank came straight on without an interval. This meant that we extra British musicians had to sit on the stage with Buddy's band so that we were in position when Frank came on. To sit in with all that sound going on around was a very thrilling experience. Buddy's solo, of course, was quite wonderful but the way he controlled the band and drove it along was really something else. We had a very good trombone section, three of them and yours truly. It was a great experience to play the Sinatra book again, this time with a young American band.

We played the Moulin Rouge in Paris to a packed house of – I would say – very wealthy people. Their reaction was rather blasé but I believe Paris audiences are notoriously difficult to please. In Vienna, we played to eleven-and-a-half thousand people – a tremendous success!

This latest Sinatra tour was another occasion when I was very glad to have been a musician.

Brass Bands

One day in 1975, a call came from Geoffrey Brand to see if I could have a meeting with him. We settled the date and I duly went to his office where I met him and Peter Wilson. I had no idea what they wanted to see me about.

Over lunch they came to the point. They wanted a new serious work for Trombone and Brass Band to be performed for the first time at the Gala Concert following the National Band Contest at The Royal Albert Hall in October. I accepted, thinking it an honour and a challenge.

Gordon Langford was to be the composer which pleased me since I admired his work so much. It was suggested that we meet to talk about it; we had plenty of time and I would then be able to see that he didn't write anything too hard!

We eventually met and spent a couple of hours going over the work he had written whilst on holiday in Spain. It was a great thrill hearing it take shape – I needn't have worried.

I took the manuscript home and started to work on it. Twice I drove down to rehearse with The Cory Band under the direction of Major Kenny. It was great fun to meet this fine group of people and they made me very welcome. Gordon Langford and Brian Cousins of Chandos Music, the publishers of the *Rhapsody,* came with me. The Cory Band were to accompany me at the concert because they had been the winning band in the previous year's contest.

The evening before the concert, there was a rehearsal for everyone at the Royal Albert Hall when we played it through just once. It felt rather strange; the sound was running all around the empty hall, we were short of space and this made the band and me uncomfortable. There were, of course, quite a lot of bandsmen in the hall but no one applauded; they just looked at us with expression of 'Come on, show us' on their faces – or so it seemed to me at the time. Then one of the organisers shouted, 'Next band, please' and we were bundled off the platform.

I began to wish I wasn't doing it; too late to turn back now though. 'Let's just see what happens tomorrow!', I kept thinking to myself.

I spent most of the contest day listening to the bands, meeting people and enjoying it all very much. The only trouble was that I kept thinking about my solo spot that evening. I had taken my trombone and clothes with me so that I could stay on without going home. But once the contest was over and the results were given out, I changed my mind about staying and I was off like a shot. I drove home and quietly played through the piece again having had a little practice first thing that morning. Now I put on my track suit and went off for a run round; then a light meal and a clean-up before driving back to the Royal Albert Hall. There is a spot I know which is away from everyone, near the boiler room. There I had a good warm up.

The 1981 Belle Vue 'Open' Championships with Don entertaining.

Sharing a dressing room with the conductors and compere John Dunn, I remember taking part in a lot of small talk when suddenly the concert started. I was very nervous and wanted to get the whole thing over. Of course, I'm used to playing in front of big audiences but this was rather different; seven-and-a-half thousand people, a new work, a live recording and the fact that I was playing to a brass band audience who would be very critical. You see, though I was brought up in brass bands and started playing in the Salvation Army when I was six, I had had no connection with brass bands for years, even though I always listened to them and followed their careers. I tried to keep calm but when I was announced and walked out on to the platform, I could hardly feel my legs. I saw that vast array of faces and that's the last thing I remember until I heard a bit of applause. I had to go back for another bow. It had gone down well – what a relief!

It turned out to be a wonderful evening and many people said kind things to me. I went along and said 'thank you' to the Cory Band and Major Kenny. A few weeks later, I drove up to Huddersfield Town Hall and recorded it for Chandos Records with Black Dyke Mills band under the direction of Roy Newsome.

The playing of that piece at the Royal Albert Hall opened up for me new avenues for, before long, I was asked to go and play it here, there and everywhere. Since then I have been all over the United Kingdom, Europe, Canada and the USA. As I write, I have been asked to go to Australia to perform it. I shall forever be grateful to Geoffrey Brand for asking me to give that first performance.

You may be interested to know that, after a time, I felt I was playing it so much that it was becoming stale, so I gave it a rest. But there were so many requests for it that I had to take it up again. It always goes down well; I enjoy hearing other people play it and I still enjoy performing it myself.

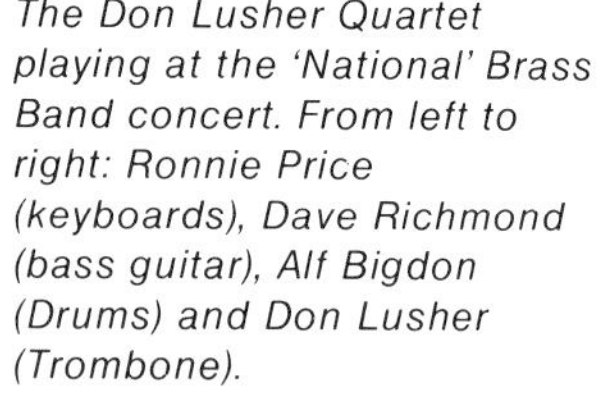

The Don Lusher Quartet playing at the 'National' Brass Band concert. From left to right: Ronnie Price (keyboards), Dave Richmond (bass guitar), Alf Bigdon (Drums) and Don Lusher (Trombone).

Television

Some years ago, Yvonne Littlewood did a television series for BBC 2 which featured famous musicians like James Galway, David Rose, Bob Farnon and Ray Charles. One day in 1979, Yvonne asked me to her office to tell me that she proposed to do a 'Don Lusher's World of Music'. Completely taken aback, we talked about the format of the show and who was going to be on it.

On the show was The Don Lusher Big Band made up of some of the best studio musicians in the world. We played modern big-band music together with a tribute to Ted Heath; within the big band was The Don Lusher Quartet.

Because I'm completely mad about trombone, we used my ten-piece trombone ensemble to play arrangements by Gordon Langford and Pete Smith. Singing with the big band and a large string section was the delightful Marti Caine, content on this occasion to not crack even one gag, but just to sing – which she did beautifully.

As part of my connection with brass bands we had The Black Dyke Mills Band conducted by Major Peter Parkes and Michael Antrobus. Apart from playing some of their own pieces they played for me in Gordon Langford's *Rhapsody for Trombone.*

To represent the American conductors for whom I work from time to time we had the great Nelson Riddle. He wrote and conducted a Barry Manilow medley for orchestra, did two arrangements for Marti Caine and an arrangement featuring the string section and me in *Here's that Rainy Day* which I still love to play.

Nelson also chatted with me; his relaxed attitude spread around the entire production. It was a great opportunity and experience for me to work with Yvonne Littlewood and her BBC production staff; I shall always be grateful to her for giving me the chance to have such a programme. The reviews

Marti Caine appearing on the BBC Television programme 'Don Lusher's World of Music' (Photography: BBC Copyright).

and the ratings were very good, thanks to the good atmosphere and everyone's hard work.

My great worry at this time came from Eileen's illness. It was touch and go whether she would be well enough to come to the show. However, as usual, she came up trumps and made it. It always seems so sad to me that she spent all the hard times together with me while she was healthy. When the really good times came she was too ill to enjoy them.

I've recently been looking through the reviews which were really appreciative. There was talk of perhaps doing a series with the Big Band and guests. Alas nothing came of it and, as time goes by, it becomes increasingly more difficult to get a band on television – or radio for that matter.

A studio scene from the 'Don Lusher's World of Music' programme. (Photography: BBC Copyright).

Friends and Colleagues

Over the years I've had the opportunity of working for and with some wonderful musicians, not only talented in their writing and conducting, but also fine people. The list would be enormous if I mentioned everyone, so I beg forgiveness to anyone who should have been mentioned and isn't.

I've had many dates with leading symphony orchestras when we have been playing for film scores or something similar and have always found excellent playing from very interesting people.

Many times when I've been standing in the wings waiting to go on at a brass band concert, I've marvelled at the playing from this bunch of characters! The same goes when I'm out doing a jazz date, with a wind band and when I'm doing studio work. Our calls can be very early in the morning, yet some players have been working very late the night before and still play well. Many times these players have much to worry about – illness, finances, domestic problems – in spite of these circumstances and many others they have turned out great performances.

I've worked with many musicians both from the USA and Europe. It's been the same the world over – always people I could look up to, learn from and admire. And not only players but also the writers and musical directors.

Before any Bob Farnon date there is always a sense of anticipation – you know it's going to be good before you start. Many times I just sit back and let those wonderful sounds wash right

Robert (Bob) Farnham conducting on his own television show, with Don Lusher soloing.

Jack Parnell, Kenny Baker and Don Lusher appearing with 'Best of British Jazz'.

over me. Some of his solo trombone writing is difficult to play but always very worthwhile. His conducting is easy to follow. As a man, he is gentle and can be very witty. At the end of most sessions he will say 'Thank you; same time, same place, next week'. Many people throughout the world refer to him as 'The Governor'.

For many years I worked with the Jack Parnell Band at the ATV Studios in Elstree. As soon as Jack gives the down beat you know exactly where to place the notes and the mood he wants the piece played in. Time and feel are very important to him and he has the knack of passing this on to the players no matter how large or small the combination.

Many times, he has guided us through fine television shows, conducting all types of music for some of the biggest names in show business. He loves a good joke and is a great story teller. His personality and appearance when fronting an orchestra are first class and, when he plays the drums, thats wonderful as well.

I work with Jack in a group called 'The Best of British Jazz', a really enjoyable and rewarding experience. The rhythm section consists of Tony Lee on piano, Tony Archer on bass and Jack Parnell on drums. In the front line, we have Kenny Baker (trumpet), Betty Smith (tenor saxophone and vocals) with me on trombone. The three front line players take it in turns to do the announcements. Kenny takes charge of the playing and I can assure you he gives Betty and myself a real work-out. Even while we are playing, he will make up riffs and gives us notes to play when we are playing background chords. Both Jack and Kenny do their own vocals so we have a good all-round show. We try to present good jazz coupled with entertainment so that, if we are playing to an audience who are not very interested in jazz we are still able to give pleasure.

We play in the smaller theatres and concert halls and sometimes out of doors to audiences of between two hundred and a thousand people. We sometimes do outside concerts for the Greater London Council in the summer.

People in the audience come with picnics and bottles of wine to sit on the grass and eat while we play. It is very good fun for everyone. One evening, a little boy of about four was running around among the audience when suddenly he saw Kenny playing a solo. He stopped in his tracks and crept up to the edge of the stage and stood spell-bound swaying in time to the music for a very long time. At one point I thought he was going to come up on stage with us; its not often one gets that kind of concentration – most gratifying!

Betty, who I have known for many years, and her husband Jack Peberdy, organise the bookings and the business side. Jack is a very fine musician; he writes for all kinds of people including brass bands. At the beginning of 1985, Betty became very ill; we are all very worried and miss her terribly in the group. Let's hope we'll all soon be back together again. The group have made two albums; one called *The Best of British Jazz* and the other *The Very Best of British Jazz*. If we make another I can't imagine what we're going to call it – we'll run out of superlatives!

Another person who comes from Peterborough is Barry Forgie. He is a really good writer and a very inspiring character to have out in front. He is a happy soul and loves a really good laugh. We were in the Salvation Army together and both play trombone. I remember his parents well for Barry is a lot younger than I am.

He went to King's School, the other grammar school in Peterborough. I remember when I went to Deacon's there was always great rivalry between the two schools. Of course, we didn't go to school at the same time.

One day, he phoned me for some advice. I was doing quite well in the music business and he was nearing the end of his college days where he had covered himself in glory. He told me that he dearly wanted to go into the music business; should he give it a try or go into teaching? In those days, teaching was a very respected and steady profession. After I had given the problem some thought, I told him to settle for teaching and maybe do a little playing on the side. I'm glad to say that he didn't take my advice. I still feel guilty about it but Barry is very good and we often have a laugh when I tell him to 'get a proper job before long!'

Nelson Riddle is always a joy to work for; his music is very exciting with wonderful sounds and rhythms and perfect orchestrations. He wrote that great score for me of *Here's that Rainy Day*, just strings, harp and me. I gather he had arranged it overnight; we rehearsed it a couple of times and then recorded the TV show the same evening. I was pleased because, in the coda, the solo part went higher and higher, finishing with a hold on high D with vibrato. Nelson walked over to me in the brake and said, 'I'm sorry, I wrote the last part of the arrangement in the wrong key; it should have been a tone down! We had a good laugh.

He came over to London in July 1984 to conduct for Ella Fitzgerald at the Grosvenor House and I was in the band. I had a beautiful solo to play in a number called *You're mine, you* originally written for the great trombone player; Murray McEachern. Nelson cuts his gestures to a minimum when he conducts and his is always very appreciative of the musicians. During this concert, he told the audience a little story about a beggar who invites all his friends to bring something to make stone soup. 'I'll bring the stones' said the beggar. 'The musicians are like all the other people bringing good things to make the soup while I only bring the stones.' It's very good to be appreciated since

Nelson Riddle and Don Lusher in party mood in Hollywood.

sometimes the musicians can be made to feel very insignificant.

Derek Jewell in the *Sunday Times*, after this concert, commented that Nelson observed that I was 'one of England's National Treasures'. It made me feel a bit like a museum piece. But I was grateful for the thought. However, Nelson explained to me much later that this is how the Japanese refer to their artists and that it is a great honour; so the phrase does not seem so strange to me now.

This reminds me of another Ella Fitzgerald and Oscar Peterson concert some time ago. Eileen, my wife, was becoming really very ill and I realised that I wouldn't have her much longer. She loved Ella Fitzgerald and I decided that I would take her to the concert. It was again at the Grosvenor House, the audience have dinner first and then watch the show from their dining tables. The seats are very expensive but I was determined that she should have this last opportunity. I was very afraid that she wouldn't be able to manage the stairs but all was well and we sat down with eight other people, none of whom we knew. The meal was excellent but neither Eileen nor I had any of our bottle of wine; Eileen, because she was too ill to drink, and I never drink before playing.

At the end of the meal, when it was time for the band to go on, I got up and, tucking our bottle of wine under one arm, beat a hasty retreat. The people at the table looked rather startled, so Eileen said, 'Oh, my husband can't stand Ella, he's gone to have a quiet drink where he can't hear her.' She was sure that when they saw the show they would see me on the stand and have a quiet laugh. But no, they didn't recognise me – which only goes to show that to many people the band is a faceless mass.

Eileen enjoyed the show tremendously and after much difficulty we made it to the car and home. She was very glad that she made the effort and had a lovely experience to look back on when she became virtually housebound.

In June 1984, I worked for Henry Mancini. He had written an album for James Galway, all the numbers being his own compositions. Some were well known like *The Pink Panther;* others specially written; one piece I well remember was called *Cameo for Flute.* I loved it and so did everyone in the orchestra. It was quite a difficult piece to play, with a lot of notes for James. We worked on it and started to record it. James really got down to work and wouldn't give up until he and everyone else was completely satisfied. His stamina was fantastic. Both James and Henry can be very funny so I can assure you that it wasn't all serious and we had a lot of laughs.

After the recording sessions we went along to the Barbican and gave two concerts, one at five and the other at eight, with a rehearsal in the morning. The first half was just Henry and the orchestra playing his own scores with some Ellington and Hoagy Carmichael medleys. The second was with James Galway playing the numbers from the new album we had just recorded. The atmosphere was magic with the playing of James and the orchestra just thrilling. It was one of those nights to remember.

After the concert Derek Jewell wrote an article about the packed houses for the two concerts which said, 'Britons like Don Lusher and Kenny Clare aglow at working under so complete a musical pro'. So our enjoyment in playing the music was also obvious to others.

In 1983, I appeared on BBC television in 'Breakfast Time' with Henry Mancini. I was promoting a brass band concert; Henry was being interviewed. I didn't know that Henry would be there and I had arranged to play *Early One Morning*, appropriate, if a little obvious. When I saw Henry, I rushed into the privacy of the toilet to organise *The Days of Wine and Roses* as a tribute to him. I was playing alone and so there was no one else to worry about. We did the show with that number; afterwards Henry said, 'That was a funny key to play it in.' I replied rather weakly, 'Well, it lays easily for the trombone in that key.' 'Really, you think I don't know that!' he replied. It was *very* early in the morning.

It's always a great joy to play for Henry. He is a giant in the art of writing beautiful melodies, all his writing is very effective. In front of an orchestra he knows all the answers with regard to getting the best results and he can be a very funny man. I've done a certain amount of solo playing for him; he is always most encouraging.

I've worked for Alan Ainsworth for many years, with big bands and the pop orchestras of to-day. He is a very good composer and arranger with a great understanding of modern music. He is as good as you will find in the use of colour and rhythmic feel. He also writes some very interesting trombone solos. He is fully in control of an orchestra and I've seen him come through some very sticky situations on live television.

We were doing a live television show from Her Majesty's Theatre one Sunday in 1984 when Tommy Cooper was into his act. Tommy started to fool about and grab the curtains, falling on to the stage. We thought he was fooling; then we heard an awful gasping and we knew he was very ill. We couldn't move and stared at Alan to see what to do. He raised his hands and we went straight into the music for the commercial break with complete control and the show went on as scheduled.

Afterwards we heard that poor Tommy had suffered a heart attack and had died. As his wife said later that was how Tommy would have liked to go – on stage with the audience laughing.

Alan Ainsworth belongs to that great tradition of performers for whom the show must go on!

Dick Nash is one of the foremost all-round trombone players in the world; I'm proud to count hims among my best friends. One time, when I was staying with him in Los Angeles, he gave me a 'practice kit.' It was comprised of a book of *Bach, Two Part Inventions* transcribed for trombone and a leader pipe in which you insert your own mouthpiece. The other end of the pipe is half closed with a piece of cork. When you play into it, the half-closed end offers about the same resistance as an average trombone.

You can do any sort of playing on this kit but it is particularly useful if, at any time, you can't get at a trombone. I've used it on planes and trains and warmed up in my car many times. I still use it with the study book.

For any of you that don't know, a leader pipe is a shank-like pipe about six to nine inches long, into which fits your mouthpiece. It is a vital part of any brass instrument.

A break during a Hollywood film recording session for (left to right) Dick Noel, George Roberts, Don Lusher, Dick Nash and Hoyt Bohannon.

It is, of course, very difficult keeping in touch over such distance; messages from American players and conductors keep coming and I write – not very frequently I admit, – but I do try to keep in contact.

Geoffrey Brand is a man with enormous drive and energy, both physical and mental. As a conductor, I have found him capable of getting tremendous results. He is a major force in the world of music especially with brass and wind bands. I get the impression that he is the head of a very united family which extends out of his home and embraces the total world of his music and business.

It was Geoffrey's idea for me to do the first performance of the Gordon Langford *Rhapsody for Trombone.* He has been very good to me and I am forever grateful.

I worked for Peter Knight on and off for many years. He was a very sensitive musician and his writing a joy to play and listen to. He was yet another musician with a great capacity for work and with tremendous stamina. Peter died in August 1985 and will be sadly missed.

Roy Newsome knows the brass band world better than anyone else. As a conductor and trainer, he has great know-how and he is capable of drawing the very best available results from any player. I find him a very real and genuine person.

Ronnie Hazlehurst's motto in life must be 'Efficiency in all things'. His writing is beautiful and always correct; as a conductor I have seen him get through some very difficult live television shows without putting a foot wrong. A really good organiser and a hard worker. I really like working for him.

Peter Parkes is yet another conductor with a great capacity for work and with a very full general knowledge of music. Both of these qualities help him with his band work both in training and conducting. He has achieved some wonderful results on the 'big day'. I enjoy working with him and have found him a most helpful person.

Another person I like to make music with is Pete Moore; his writing is always just right and he gets some fine sounds, whatever the combination. He writes good passages for trombones and is always keen to help with any problem, musical or personal.

The first time I played for Wally Stott was a very big thrill indeed. His writing is as good as you will find anywhere in the world. The attention to detail in performance is very great and yet always achieved with the minimum amount of effort. I still have many of his arrangements for the Heath Band. Some time ago, Wally decided to become Angela Morley and has continued to write just as beautifully under that name as she did under the old one. Since Angela has been working and living in the USA, we have all missed her no end. I still work for her when she is in the UK and I still get a big thrill from doing so. She is tremendously respected by fellow musicians; this is obvious that moment she starts to conduct. Every session with her is a joy for me.

Harry Rabinowitz seems to have one of the quickest brains I have ever known. It is very important to be extremely alert when he is giving out instructions. He has a quick wit and is a very well schooled musician. Life is never dull when you work for Harry.

Jerry Fielding must be one of the cleverest musicians that I have worked for. Unfortunately he is no longer with us and we all miss him. He could sometimes be scathing with his comments but also appreciative when it was called for. He was a fast worker and a hard one; maybe too hard.

From the ranks of the Salvation Army, I have chosen to mention Colonel Bernard Adams. I can remember going to see the International Staff Band with my father. Bernard was then solo cornet; I was very impressed not only with his playing but by his personality. Of course, I have never played under him but I have seen him conduct the ISB and I would say that when he takes the baton he is magic. At times when I am playing at the Fairfield Hall, Croydon, he will come round to the back and have a chat with me. I consider it a great honour that he takes the trouble to do this.

I have admired Kai Winding since the old Stan Kenton days. Later on I heard him play and met him on several occasions. About six years ago, he asked me to join him in a trombone combo and I was very thrilled. We did a couple of tours together using a British rhythm section. We also did a BBC 2 programme produced by Ken Griffin called 'Jazz on 2'. I have a video of this programme so I can still see and hear Kai now he is no longer with us. During the time I was working with him, I learned so much not only about playing and improvisation, but about many other things such as programme planning, dress and 'taking care of business' (His phrase, not mine!) We lived and travelled together; both he and his wife Eleanor became great friends.

At the end of the last tour we did together, Eileen was dying slowly but surely. Eleanor was Kai's second wife; his first wife died many years ago leaving him alone with his daughters to bring up. He was able to comfort me and help me a great deal as he had been through the same experience. In fact, I doubt very much whether I would have got through that tour without his support. His death is a terrible loss to us all. Eleanor told me that he left quite a lot of unpublished music. I do hope she succeeds in getting it published; it would be a loss to the world if it were not.

Kenny Baker is a person I have admired for many years. He has such a strong personality which comes out in his playing. His impact on an audience is amazing and he is greatly admired by his fellow musicians. He makes it all look so easy but I know that he still does a great deal of work to achieve those results. Music apart, he is a clever man, a great 'Do-It-Yourself' enthusiast and has a great zest for living. I am proud to work with him and to be one of his friends. He's taught me a great deal – and not only about music!

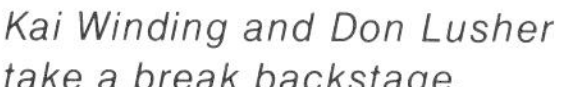

Kai Winding and Don Lusher take a break backstage.

Travel

One of the perks of being a musician is the opportunity to travel. Sometimes, of course, it can become too much but, by and large, it has been a wonderful experience. Both of my sons, David and Philip, have also been able to come travelling, either with me or on their own account as musicians. David was very lucky in working in the Far East, seeing Hong Kong, Singapore, Bangkok and Kuala Lumpar. Musicians often work and stay in some of the best hotels in the world, far better than one would be able to afford oneself. You can catch a glimpse of how the other half lives!

Here is just a small selection from some of the trips which have left the biggest impressions on me.

In 1955 the Ted Heath Band went to Australia and New Zealand, stopping off in the USA on the way back. It took just one month. The journey was a great deal longer than it is to-day; we had bad engine trouble at Karachi and were delayed by two days. Consequently we arrived by Super Constellation in Sydney two hours before a concert was due to start.

When we arrived at the hotel, they wouldn't let us in because we weren't wearing ties and had to start searching through our suitcases to find them. You can imagine the panic. Fortunately, we had had a trumpet and trombone on the plane and had been tootling one by one throughout the journey; otherwise there would not have been much of a concert! The band went down very well in Australia. We enjoyed the sunshine and made many friends.

From 1956 onwards, the same band did several trips to the USA, sometimes the long journeys by air, road and rail, could be hard, but it was always interesting. It was good to meet so many musicians from the States and the band went down well everywhere.

1975, saw me on a trip to Japan, as part of an orchestra of twenty five players lead by John Barry. We had been working for him doing the music for the James Bond films and, when he was asked to do this tour, he said that he would only go if he could use the same studio musicians. Eventually it was organised and we set off on New Year's day. The tour was over a period of five to six weeks, Eileen was not well and I was reluctant to leave her, but she

Bobby Lamb, Ray Premru and Don Lusher eating well in Monte Carlo before a Frank Sinatra concert.

insisted as she felt this would be a wonderful experience for me, which indeed it was.

Sid Margo was our contractor and manager and did a really fine job. The organisation was first class and we all had a wonderful time. We started off in Tokyo. We then went right down to the south of the country and then back to Tokyo. We then went right up the north returning to Tokyo before returning to London. Travel was by air and bullet-train, also a little by coach.

The band was excellent, we had a really interesting time musically and socially. We brought home many beautiful souvenirs. Japan made a big impression on us, everything was so well organised, the country and people were so different from England. I felt perfectly at home.

There is an organisation called the International Trombone Association which for one week a year takes over a college in Nashville, USA. There are around three hundred trombone students who pay to live in the college, receive tuition and take part in various concerts and activities. They are from all over the world and their ages range from eighteen to the mid-seventies. In fact, one student, a retired surgeon, had sold his instrument when he left college to buy his surgical instruments, then his surgical instruments, when he retired, to buy another trombone. Full circle!

There is a faculty of about twenty of the best trombone players in the world who are invited to attend and are paid for their services. This entails master-classes and recitals in the various concerts in all types of music, jazz, classical and through to the *avant garde.* I was invited to be on the faculty twice, once in 1980 and then again in 1982. It was a great experience to mix with not only the students but to work and live with so many wonderful players. When I was there some of my colleagues were Wayne Andre, George Roberts, Bill Watrous, Phil Wilson, Jim Pugh, and many others. Mind you, by the end of the week, you've had enough. The day starts at eight in the morning and you are on and off working until 11 at night.

In 1984, I did another trip to Australia, this time for the International Trombone Association, Australian Branch. It was held at Canberra and was roughly the same format as in Nashville. Some of the trombone players on the faculty were Phil Wilson, Miles Anderson, Rudolf Josel and Irwin Wagner, International President of the ITA. How interesting it was to be with the students gathered together from such far flung

Touring Japan with the John Barry Orchestra, Tokyo, 1975.

Band Leader Si Zentner with Don Lusher in Las Vegas.

Bert Herrick, a wonderful instrument repairer in Hollywood.

places all over Australia. When that was finished in Canberra, I went off, this time by myself, to give concerts and master classes in Melbourne, Adelaide and Sydney. I was away for two-and-a-half busy and interesting weeks.

Apart from these big trips, I have been around in Europe and the near East. One trip was with Frank Sinatra, who was giving a large charity show in Cairo, Egypt. We were playing just outside the city in the desert and beside the Sphinx. What a setting! They laid carpet over the sand to act as a stage. We rehearsed in the afternoon and everyone in the orchestra had trouble with the tremendous heat. The fiddles kept breaking strings and they were afraid that the bellies of the violins would break open. Frank was very understanding and we cut the rehearsal short. The one hour show was timed for midnight so whilst the guests, who were made up of the most distinguished and wealthy people of Cairo, were still having their dinner, the orchestra of seventy five had to take their places on the makeshift stage in complete darkness. Believe me, in the desert it really goes dark – inky black. It wasn't easy but we made it.

At midnight, the lights blazed out and the show started with a bang. The orchestra and the Sphinx were floodlit so that it was quite magical to be playing in the desert under the stars. It must have looked marvellous for the audience too. Unfortunately before long a wind sprang up and we had problems keeping the music on the stands. Happily, it was not enough to disturb the sand. Anyway, the concert was a great success but not many of us escaped the terrible 'gippo tummy' and were 'very off' for quite a few days afterwards. Put it down to experience.

I'm very glad to have had the chance to travel so extensively; good and bad experiences have all been worthwhile.

Nashville, 1980. Trombonists Phil Wilson, Don Lusher and Bill Watrous relaxing in the rest room.

A trombone ensemble playing at the International Trombone Workshop, Nashville, 1982.

Lewis Van Haney, Don Lusher and his wife, Diana preparing for Don's Master Class.

Family

Eileen and I had been married for just over thirty-three years when she died on March 27th, 1981. We had raised two sons, David and Philip, and been through a great deal, both good and bad times, together.

My son David was born in 1950. He was, and still is, in many ways, a real boy. He's a keen sportsman and a talented musician, playing guitar, singing and composing some of his own songs. He worked with his brother Philip for a time, after training at the Vidal Sassoon School of Hairdressing as a stylist. He is now in partnership with his own salon in Surbiton. Like his mother he is a diabetic, but with the better controls that the medical profession now have, he is very healthy and it seems to make very little difference to his life.

He married Tina in 1982 and for a time had a group with Tina and her twin sister Sharon which travelled all over the world. In fact, we said that they had a two-year honeymoon; they were always either just going or just coming back from some exotic place.

My younger son, Philip was born in 1953 and married Hilary in 1981. They were very sorry that the wedding was held after Eileen died so that she wasn't able to be there. Hilary has a son, Jonathan, by the previous marriage. Philip was always good with the cricket bat, and at a very early age decided that it was easier to swim under water than on top of it! He has a real talent for composing and plays several instruments, keyboards, bass, six-string guitar and drums.

He decided to go into the retail musical instrument business and is doing very well as manager of a large shop in Surbiton. I suspect the serious business of being married made him decide that a steady job was necessary. He still plays gigs in the evenings as a duo with his friend Phil. He is gifted with a somewhat sharp sense of humour, with me often at the receiving end!

At the moment Phil has cancer but is fighting hard and there is a very good chance that he will make a full recovery. Neither of my two sons gave Eileen or myself any serious cause for worry, and in many ways I wish I had had more time at home to be with them both when they were children.

In the early days of our marriage, there was very little money, but we both pulled together and were very happy. As time went by, my career started to build and life for the family became more comfortable. Eileen always supported me in every way. Sad to say she was dogged by very poor health for many years, not only diabetically but in other ways. Because of this we were never able to really enjoy our life when we had more money and the boys were off our hands. I shall always think of her with great love and respect as the wife I knew and for the courage with which she faced her long and often painful illness.

Some time after Eileen died, pianist Ronnie Price and his wife Jo asked me over for a quiet dinner. They also

Diana with son Miles.

asked Diana Kevin, a long-term friend of Jo's; Of course, I knew Diana from my Elstree days and by this time she had been divorced from Bobby Kevin, the drummer, for several years. I realised that I would like to renew our acquaintance and asked her out for dinner the following week.

We were married a few months later. I am very lucky that Diana is mature enough to realise that although I love her, I also can never forget Eileen and sometimes still grieve for her.

Sharing life with Diana is very good; she has a great capacity for work and besides looking after our home and the various inmates therein she keeps an eye on her parents living nearby, helps anyone that needs a hand, runs her own music shop and works in television as a freelance Production Assistant. She has a wonderful relationship with my sons and their families and we see quite a lot of each other.

She has a good sense of humour and we laugh a lot together. I think that you can sum up the situation by saying that the least important person in Diana's life is herself. I'm lucky aren't I?

As part of the package with Diana came her son, Miles, some furniture, one dog and an elderly cat.

My stepson Miles (born 1966) is good-looking, full of charm. His friends both male and female come to the house accompanied by loud pop-music, cigarette smoke and the smell of fast take-away food. They tell me that all this is good for me and will keep me young! Well, I'm all for that! But

Don and Diana on their wedding day with his sons, David and Philip.

"Name That Tune" Ronnie Price, who was Don's best man.

how I wish they'd not dig holes in the gravel with their car tyres.

Miles has reached that important stage in his life where he has to decide what career to go for. Many hours are spent discussing this. What a hard time young people have today with all these exams they seem to have to pass before they can get going. He'll be fine though, I'm sure.

The Christmas after we were married, Diana gave me a Siamese kitten called Holly. This, together with the elderly cat Sammy and brown dog Sheba, makes up our family.

Don working at home in his studio. (Photography Christine Murray Studio).

Recording with Johnny Mercer. Left to right: Ken Goldie, Don Lusher, Bobby Lamb, Ric Kennedy, Chris Pine and Bill Geldard.

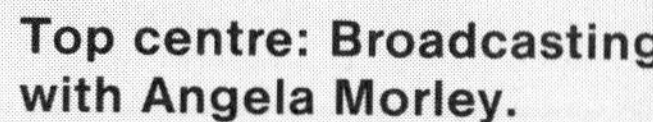

Top centre: Broadcasting with Angela Morley.

In 1976 Don received the 'Musician of the Year' award from the BBC Jazz Society. (Photograph: Roy Morris).

Don entertains a class of Suzuki students.

Recording for Gareth Wood. Left to right: Gareth Wood, Harold Nash, Don Lusher, Denis Wick and Ray Premru.

With trombonist Vic Dickenson at the Alexandra Palace, 1979. (Photograph: Denis J. Williams).

Above: Rehearsing with The Locke Brass at The Queen Elizabeth Hall, London.
Below: At the Decca recording studios, London, recording with Harry James. Left to right: Gregg Bowen, Tony Fisher, Don Lusher, Stan Rodrick, Maurice Pratt and Harry James.

Working with American trumpet virtuoso Doc Severenson at Olympic Studios, London. Left to right: Jackie Armstrong, Doc Severenson, Don Lusher and Alfie Reece.

Hints and Exercises

This part of the book is made up of both hints and exercises which I have found to be most helpful to me over my long years as a trombone player.

It can be used for all types of trombone playing. I have to assume that you know the rudiments of playing and music, but after that I am sure that it can be of help to you.

My career has brought me some wonderful experiences, having had the opportunity to meet, listen to and, in some cases, play with, some of the finest trombone players in the world such as Tommy Dorsey in 1956. Of course we 'talked trombones' and some of the hints picked up I shall now pass on to you.

This book can be used in conjunction with other study books and I do hope that you find it beneficial and enjoyable.

B&H

Contents

The Holding Position and Posture

From time to time I see trombone players with poor posture and holding the instrument badly. Players don't need to be regimented but there is a correct way of doing things. (Incidentally, speaking of regimentation I still get a great thrill whenever I see and hear one of our Guards' bands on the march headed by that wonderful line of fellow trombone players.)

The first point is that all the weight of the trombone should be taken by the left hand. The thumb goes around the bell stay, the index finger rests on the shank just below where the mouthpiece enters the mouthpipe, the remaining three fingers envelope the slide stay. This seems a nicely balanced hold.

The grip should be firm but not too tight. The right hand has an important job of not only holding the slide but also moving it to its various positions. Hold the slide stay between the thumb and index finger, the other fingers will then naturally rest against the index finger, don't try to wrap them around the slide. Here again the hold should be firm but not too tight.

I think that the movement of the slide should be in a gliding manner; you will certainly have to move fast but try not to make the movement too jerky. If you do, this type of movement can reflect in your playing.

Try not to get too much free movement from the wrist as this can make the playing rather sloppy and, of course, inaccurate. I find it best to keep the hand and forearm as one and let the movement come from the elbow, rather like a hinge.

I don't really wish to lay down any rules about the angle the instrument should be at, I don't like to have it pointed down too much towards the ground, as this interferes with my breathing and air passage. Likewise you don't have to point it towards the sky. Somewhere between horizontal and down a few degrees is good for general playing. By the way, whilst we are on the subject of angles, you can achieve good effects either with the section or for solo playing by either pointing down, when the sound from out front will be quite muffled, or by pointing up a little, when the sound will come out over the heads of the audience. So often we seem to be hindered by those oversized music stands.

A couple of points about posture. If you are sitting, sit upright with your lower back well into the chair-back. Please don't sit cross-legged. (You could do yourselves an injury fellows! This problem does not apply to our lady players). And try not to curl your legs around the chair legs.

When you are standing, be upright. I prefer to have my legs a little apart as this distributes the weight evenly. For both sitting and standing, be upright to allow the maximum amount of air to enter the lungs but try not to be rigid and tense.

I've laid down all these points as a guide but have not wish for us all to look alike and wooden. If you feel that another way of holding the trombone is more comfortable for you, then do that. The trombone and the player should look natural and be as one.

The Position of the Mouthpiece on the Embouchure

This very controversial matter can be summed up by saying that it should be as near to the centre of the mouth as possible.

The embouchure is a highly complicated set of muscles and does a wonderful job for brass players. We are all individuals; and our teeth and jaw formations are all different. This means that we can't all achieve the best results by having the mouthpiece in the same position.

Many players play with the mouthpiece in the centre but with two thirds on the top lip and one third on the bottom lip. Others use the reverse; centre but with one third top, two thirds bottom. Again some people play off-centre, to the left or to the right. Because we are all individuals and have some natural talent, we should use the spot which is most comfortable and where we can get the best results.

Here is a way to try this out:

Place the mouthpiece in the centre and try to play a few notes using very little pressure. Now do the same in the centre but with two thirds top, one third bottom. Repeat with one third top, two thirds bottom. Without changing the pressure gradually move the mouthpiece around your embouchure, going off-centre and all over the place within reason. Stop, of course, before the mouthpiece reaches your ears.

Make a mental note of where you achieved the best results; repeat the routine several times. If you are studying with a teacher, I'm sure he will help you with this important point.

Now that you have found 'the' spot, forget about the others and really concentrate on this position.

A word of caution: I have known many cases where a player has been using a position for some time, even making steady progress. Someone has then advised that position is wrong and he should change it. The results have sometimes been very bad and even disastrous. Some young students have become so discouraged that they have stopped playing altogether. This is a terrible shame. It's a big responsibility to change an embouchure; try to obtain the very best advice possible.

Incidentally, I use a mouthpiece position of centre and one third top lip, two thirds bottom. I can't really play any other way.

When you are playing, think of the shape of your embouchure as if you were going to whistle. Pull the sides (the corners) of the mouth down slightly so that the top lip does not stretch or smile.

Don't blow your cheeks out — you don't need to.

Don't use too much pressure.

I'm sure we could all mention some big-name players who achieve wonderful results but who play off-centre with puffed-out cheeks and generally with a look of great discomfort. Well, what can we say about that? Live and let live! But please do try all the points in this chapter first before you resort to the other more unorthodox ways.

Production and Tone

Probably the most important part of trombone playing is *sound.* It doesn't matter how fast you can play, how high or low; if the quality of sound is poor — all is lost.

Don't forget, to many of the general public the trombone is still a music hall joke. A lady once asked me what I did for a living. I replied that I was a musician. 'Oh, really', she said, 'What instrument do you play?' 'The trombone', I replied. 'Oh, yes', she said, 'That's that funny thing that goes in and out!' At such times, we have to count to ten before making any comment. We must do our best to make people eat their words.

Try to listen to the best trombone players in the world; get their sound into your head. You must know what sort of sound you want to make before you try to produce it yourself. Try to make it a full sound, round but not dull, bright but not brash. Aim for a sound with life in it even when playing *pp.*

Try to add a little golden edge to the tone.

The trombone is capable of a very wide dynamic range. We must be careful to maintain this tone throughout the range. The same applies to the playing of rapid passages; good tone is not only for melodic playing; pay attention to it at all times.

* * *

A good way to practice tone production is to play any note in the middle register for a count of four slow beats, listen to the sound carefully.

I sometimes practice in front of a mirror where I can not only see what is happening to my embouchure and posture but the mirror seems to reflect the really true sound; therefore any impurities — such as gurgles or escaping air — can be heard easily.

When doing this exercise make sure that you have placed the mouthpiece on the embouchure in the position where you can produce the best quality of sound. Take a full breath; remember the chapter on breathing. Give the note a good start, not with an accent; (refer to the chapter on tonguing). Check that your sound is not pinched or thin; the latter can be caused by smiling or stretching the top lip. Both are bad habits. Make yourself aware of trying to pull down the corners of the mouth slightly. Imagine the line which a Mexican type of moustache follows; this will help you not to smile or stretch your top lip.

Now repeat the same note many times and listen all the time. When you are satisfied that all is well, move on to other notes extending the range.

Play some scales, gradually increasing the speed, vary your dynamic range, remember to listen all the time.

* * *

Playing a melody, a song or a hymn tune, pays dividends. Think of your sound all the time.

Exercise 1. (Bass Clef)

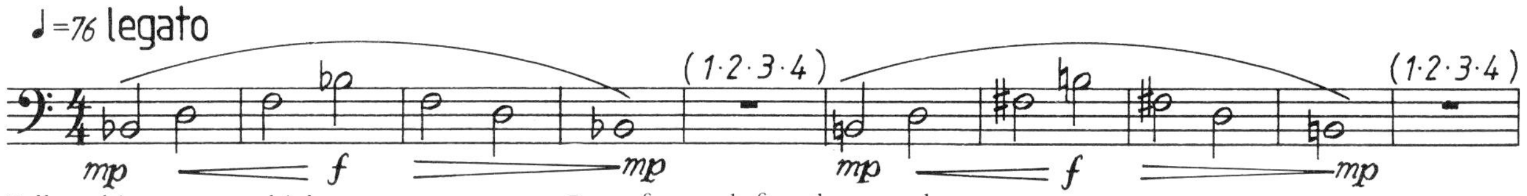

♩=76 legato

(1·2·3·4) (1·2·3·4)

mp f mp mp f mp

Follow this pattern as high as you can Rest after each fourth example

Exercise 2.

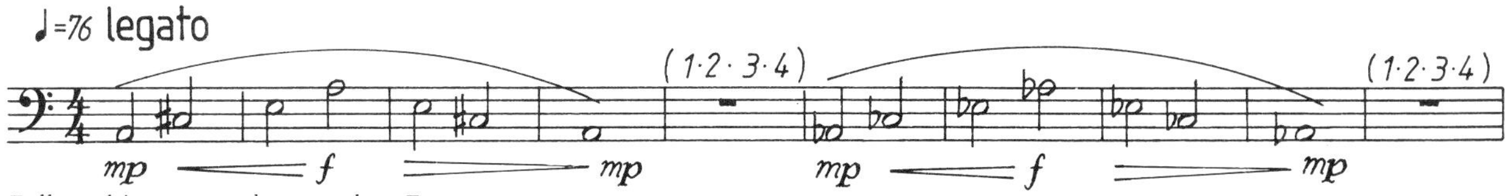

♩=76 legato

(1·2·3·4) (1·2·3·4)

mp f mp mp f mp

Follow this pattern down to low E

Finish with

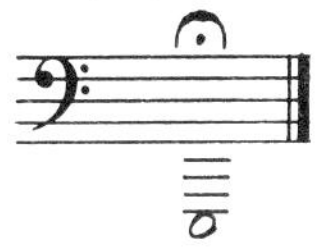

Exercise 1. (Treble Clef)

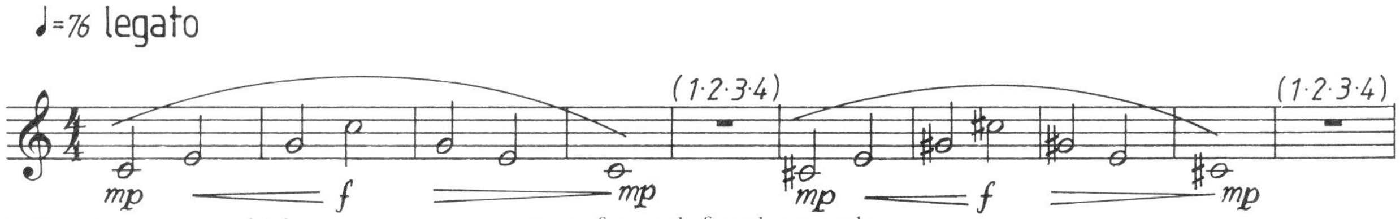

♩=76 legato

(1·2·3·4) (1·2·3·4)

mp f mp mp f mp

Follow this pattern as high as you can Rest after each fourth example

Exercise 2.

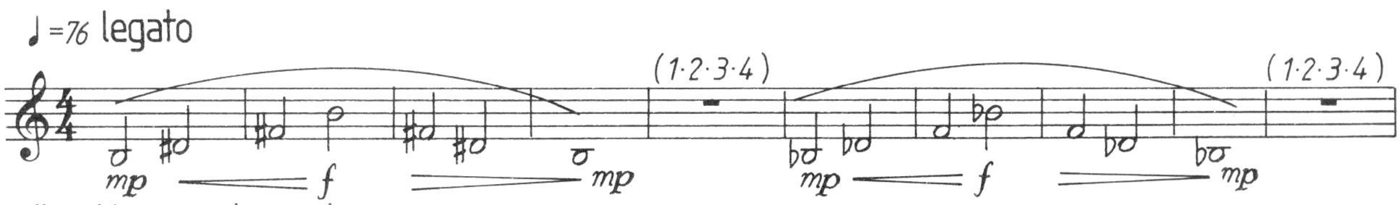

♩=76 legato

(1·2·3·4) (1·2·3·4)

mp f mp mp f mp

Follow this pattern down to low F

Finish with

8va

Music illustrations by Martin Smith

Buzzing and Mouthpiece Practice

It can be very beneficial to do some practice not only without the instrument but also without the mouthpiece; in other words practise using only the embouchure. Lips should be closed and relaxed; take a breath; blow the air through the lips. They will vibrate and make a sound. By tightening and slackening the lips, try to produce some notes. You will soon improve. Repeat this with the mouthpiece and then with the instrument.

It is surprising how many brass players don't do this; it is a shame because this method can show up defects in both the production and articulation. Everything that you can play on the instrument, you should be able to play just on the mouthpiece or the embouchure alone. If you practise this, it will eventually make everything on the instrument seem that much easier and better.

The points to remember are:
(a) Breathe well.
(b) Make certain that your embouchure position is just the same as when you are playing with the instrument.

If you are using this method as part of your warm-up, just do a few simple exercises, some single notes, flexibilities and tonguing.

Do the same exercises now with the mouthpiece. If you place a finger over about half of the hole at the end of the shank, it will make the resistance seem similar to playing with the instrument. Experiment with this until you get the right feel. (See page 55 re Dick Nash's leader pipe).

For general practice, you can try over anything that you would do on the instrument.

From time to time, check your pitch against a piano or your instrument. A good idea is to play a single note and, whilst you sustain it, gradually take the mouthpiece out of the instrument. Keep playing. Now take the mouthpiece away from the embouchure. Again keep it playing. Now replace the mouthpiece into the instrument. The buzz or vibration should keep going all the time; do your best to keep the pitch from varying.

I not only use this in general practice but also in the car on my way to a concert as a warm up. I've often thought how very funny it must look to other motorists.

The Warm Up

This is a very important part of trombone playing; it is a gradual process of preparing yourself and your trombone for either performance or for more extensive playing.

I am amazed when I see a brass player get the instrument out of the case and blast off, both loud and high, right from cold. Maybe it will all work for a few minutes, but before long the embouchure will feel terrible and then if you have to play something soft and high, as we do on trombone from time to time, then you are in real trouble. I have known the embouchure to give trouble for two or three hours in these circumstances, or even for the rest of the day.

You see, being a first class trombone player is rather like being a top athlete. You don't see runners go flat out right away. They warm to it. Our training has to be thorough and part of it has to be gradual warm ups.

Be careful to have ample breaks and rests during your warm up.

There are many pet ways of warming up but this is the sort of thing that I aim for.

First, I do a little gentle buzzing just with my lips; see the chapter on buzzing and mouthpiece practice.

Now a little break

(Maybe I assemble the trombone at this time and see that everything is working well.)

Now some gentle buzzing with the mouthpiece.

Take another short rest.

(Phone the girlfriend — quick call — no chatting.)

Now with the trombone I play a middle B flat or F below (concert) for four slow beats with a count of four beats rest in between. I play them very softly and don't use any tongue, just blow the note, see the chapter on tonguing. Page 83.

After another short break

(Feed the dog).

I will do some very simple flexibilities, just between two and three notes and still in the middle register. By this time you should feel the embouchure beginning to work.

Another short break.

(Pay the tax bill!)

Now on to some simple tongueing.

Play three notes in the middle register similar to the ones used in your flexibility warm up, then to the count of a slow four play a bar of crotchets and then rest a bar. Do this several times and then repeat this pattern with quavers and then semiquavers.

Have another rest.

(Clean shoes).

It's time now to do a few long notes, again in the middle register, with a crescendo and diminuendo. See that you count diligently and rest a little between each one. During this time you should have been paying attention to your breathing, embouchure position, sound and tonguing position. You can now extend these exercises to enlarge the range and dynamics. Work in a few scales so as to get some slide movement.

Don't forget that this is not your general practise, it is just a preparation for general playing.

My time for this can vary between ten minutes and one hour according to the circumstances. Whatever the time available is, still take your breaks and adjust the routine to fit in with the time at your disposal. *At the end of your warm up, play a series of pedal B flats; this will help to relax your embouchure.*

The warm up is vital to good brass playing.

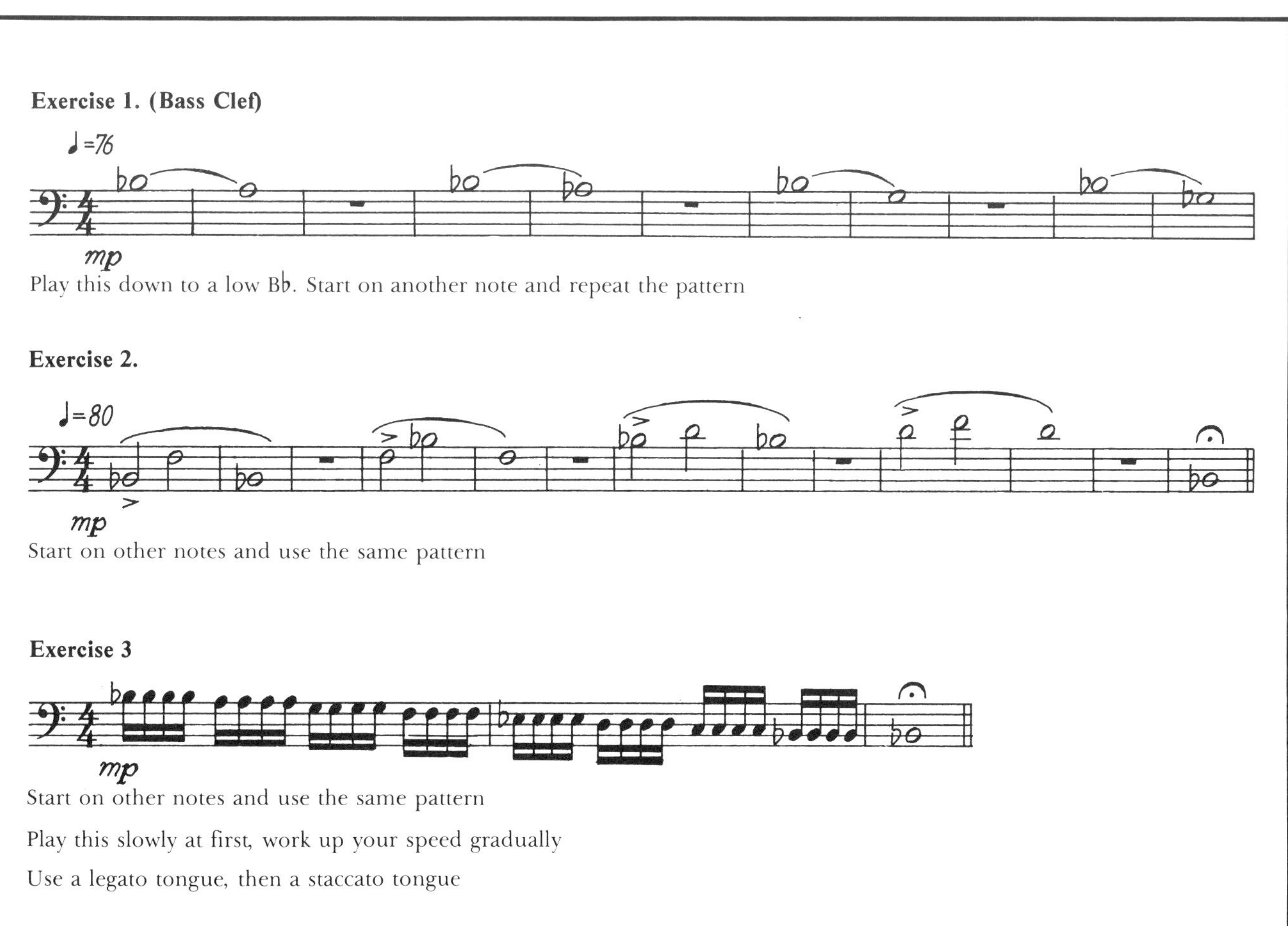

Exercise 1. (Treble Clef)

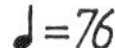

Play this down to a low C. Start on another note and repeat the pattern

Exercise 2.

Start on other notes and use the same pattern

Exercise 3.

Start on other notes and use the same pattern

Play this slowly at first, work up your speed gradually

Use a legato tongue, then a staccato tongue

Projection

This is a subject which to me is very important; it also seems to have been overlooked somewhat in the past.

Try to see it this way: if your air stream stops or falters, something will go wrong with the note. Your sound is made from the vibration of your lips and then sent on its way by means of a column of moving air. It is as simple as that!

I always try to think of the air column going in at the mouthpiece, going right round the tubing, out of the bell and then on to the very back of the room in which I am playing.

Now this does not mean that I am thinking in terms of a great blast of sound. Not at all. Its just as important when playing quietly — in fact even more so — for that is when so often we can run into trouble with faltering notes.

So try and be aware of it all the time, take in the breath and steadily push it through the instrument and right to the back of the room. Don't just play into your instrument; play through it!

This exercise will help you.

Exercise 1. (Treble Clef)

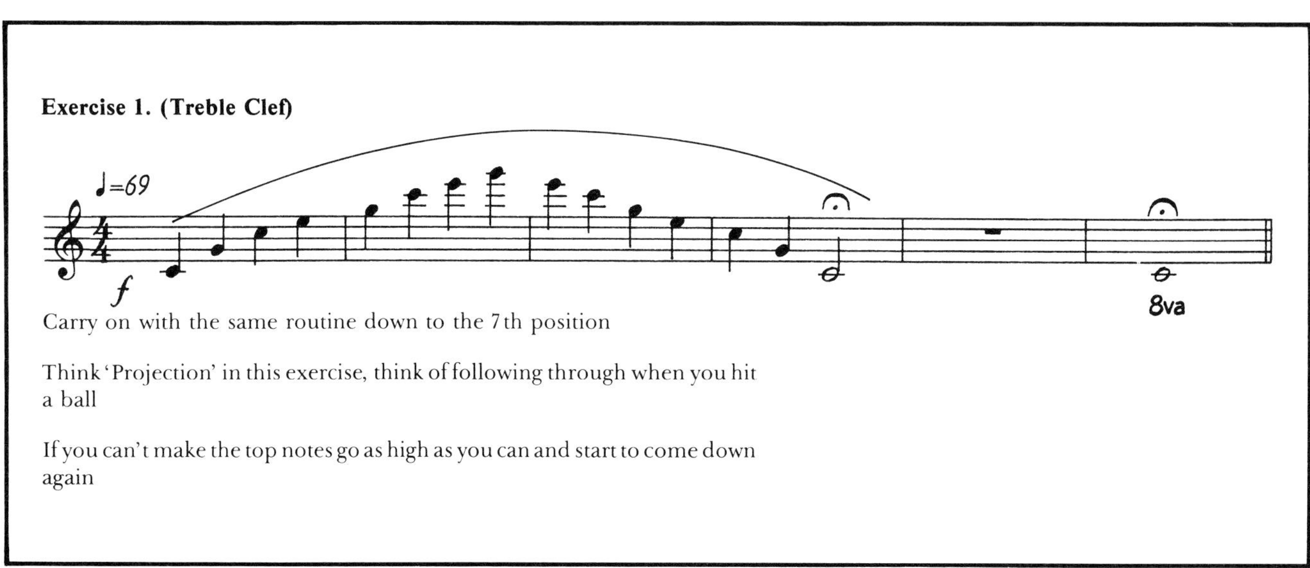

Carry on with the same routine down to the 7th position

Think 'Projection' in this exercise, think of following through when you hit a ball

If you can't make the top notes go as high as you can and start to come down again

Tonguing

The most important thing to realise about tonguing is that the tongue, which should be placed somewhere at the back of the top set of teeth, stops the air supply going through the embouchure to the instrument. Without that air supply, the embouchure cannot vibrate and, of course, without those vibrations we have no sound. Once we have quickly withdrawn our tongue the air supply can pass through, the embouchure will vibrate and we have a sound.

A word concerning the position of the tongue. I think we must make room for a little individuality. I have known players achieve very good results by placing the tongue anywhere in between the roof of the mouth and where the lips meet, but not going through the lips. Make sure that wherever the tongue position is, you have a good air-tight seal. After taking a breath, the air stream should be continuous, controlled only by the movement of the tongue, open and closed.

Just as the note is being made, a gentle push upwards with the diaphragm should be made. It is possible to produce notes without using the tongue, to use only the push upwards from the diaphragm can be very good practise.

Use the syllable TEE for high register, TOO for the middle register and TA for the lower register.

When playing legato, I think of stroking the notes, also using the syllables, DEE for high, DOO for middle and DA for the lower notes.

Practise single notes and then go on to some scales. When you are satisfied that everything is working well, proceed to more advanced studies. Do plenty of melodic lines to help with your *legato* playing. Think S-M-O-O-T-H at all times.

Now on to fast single tonguing. I have to say that I know some players find this harder than others. The best method of improving single tonguing, to my mind, is:

First, remember all I've said so far about tonguing; then play a bar of semiquavers, all on the same middle register note. Select a comfortable tempo, rest for a bar and repeat, but this time play the bar a little faster.
Gradually extend this to four bars and increase the tempo all the time.
Play the notes both *staccato* and *legato*, and with various dynamics.
Proceed with some scalic patterns and so on to some difficult passages. *Never sacrifice clean articulation for speed.*

* * *

Double tonguing

This can be a great asset. It is possible to work up speeds which will be in excess of a good, fast single tongue. The mechanism of the tongue is TA - KAH, the KAH action is done by the back of the tongue, the TA is as for normal single tonguing.

It is a good idea to practise a series of notes just using the KAH; try and match the sound up to the TA.

After spending some time on this, do some single notes using the syllables TA-KAH; then on to some scalic patterns. Keep the speed very slow and then gradually build it up. Always aim for clarity.

This kind of practise can sound terrible, but don't be put off — it will improve.

It is possible to obtain good results by using similar syllables such as DU-GUH. As with single tonguing, as you progress move on to more advanced studies.

Keep a good air supply moving through the instrument; aim for a very even sound and neatness at all times.

* * *

Triple Tonguing

Before I go into the technique of triple tonguing, may I advise you to listen to soloists in the brass band world, many of whom perform this type of tonguing as well as anyone in the world. If you have problems with your triple tonguing try and have a word with one of these players; I'm sure you'll find it a great help.

The tongue action is TA TA KAH or TA KAH TA; as in double tonguing the syllables can be changed to DU DU GAH.

The method of practise should be as for double tonguing; slowly at first — speed will eventually come.

* * *

Doodle Tonguing

This is used by some of the greatest jazz players in the world. It will mean that once you have it mastered you should be able to play your jazz solos just as fast as any trumpet or saxophone player.

The tongue action is DOO ELL or a slight variation of this.

The practice formula should be as for the other forms of tonguing. It is very important that the slide and tonguing movement really co-ordinate, so do plenty of scale practise.

I feel with this type of tonguing, best results are obtained when playing fairly softly. It is very effective used in conjunction with a good microphone technique.

It is a good idea to do a certain amount of tonguing practice just with the embouchure as with buzzing, then with the mouthpiece and finally with the instrument.

Flexibility

There are certain points with regard to flexibility which we must try and do all the time. They are:

Use plenty of air and make sure your air stream is strong.

Keep the embouchure steady; no smiling. My tongue position will vary according to the range I am playing in.

I use the syllable TOO-EE and TEE-OO to move up and down.

Don't force it.

I'm sure that you will find time spent on these and other flexibility studies beneficial; it is such an important part of all-round trombone playing.

Listen to other players who are very good at this sort of playing.

Exercise 4. (Bass Clef)

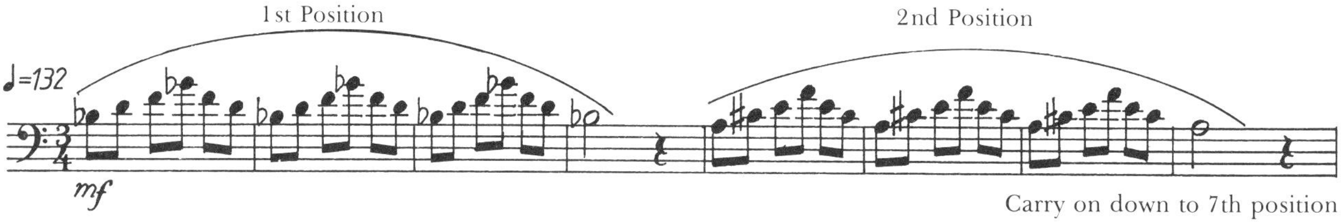

1st Position — 2nd Position

♩=132

mf

Carry on down to 7th position

Take a rest

Exercise 5.

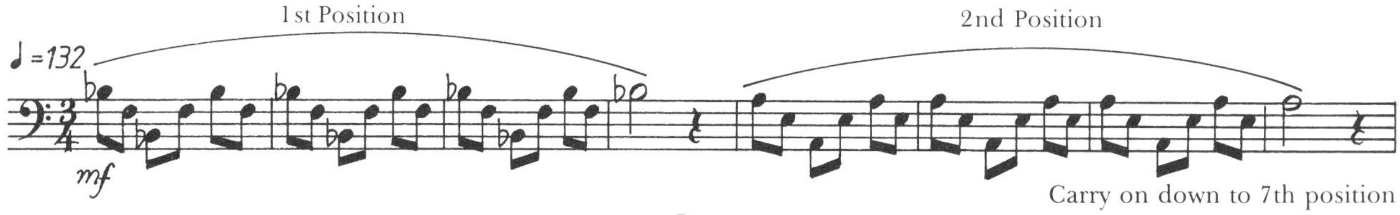

1st Position — 2nd Position

♩=132

mf

Carry on down to 7th position

Rest

Exercise 6.

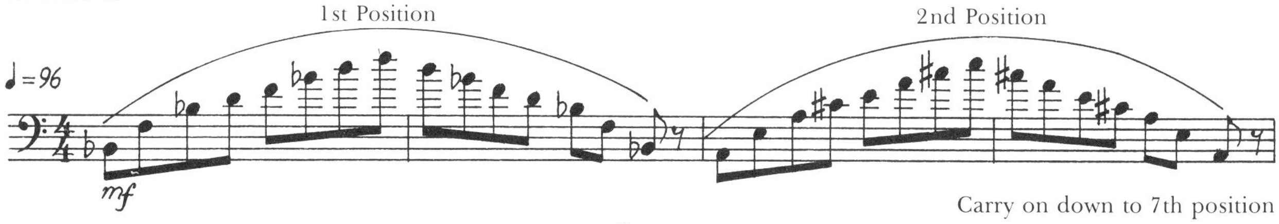

1st Position — 2nd Position

♩=96

mf

Carry on down to 7th position

Rest

Exercise 7.

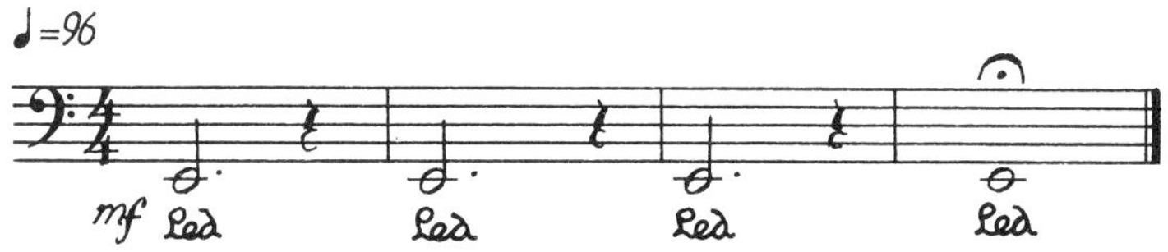

♩=96

mf Ped. Ped. Ped. Ped.

You may alter the speed and dynamics as you wish

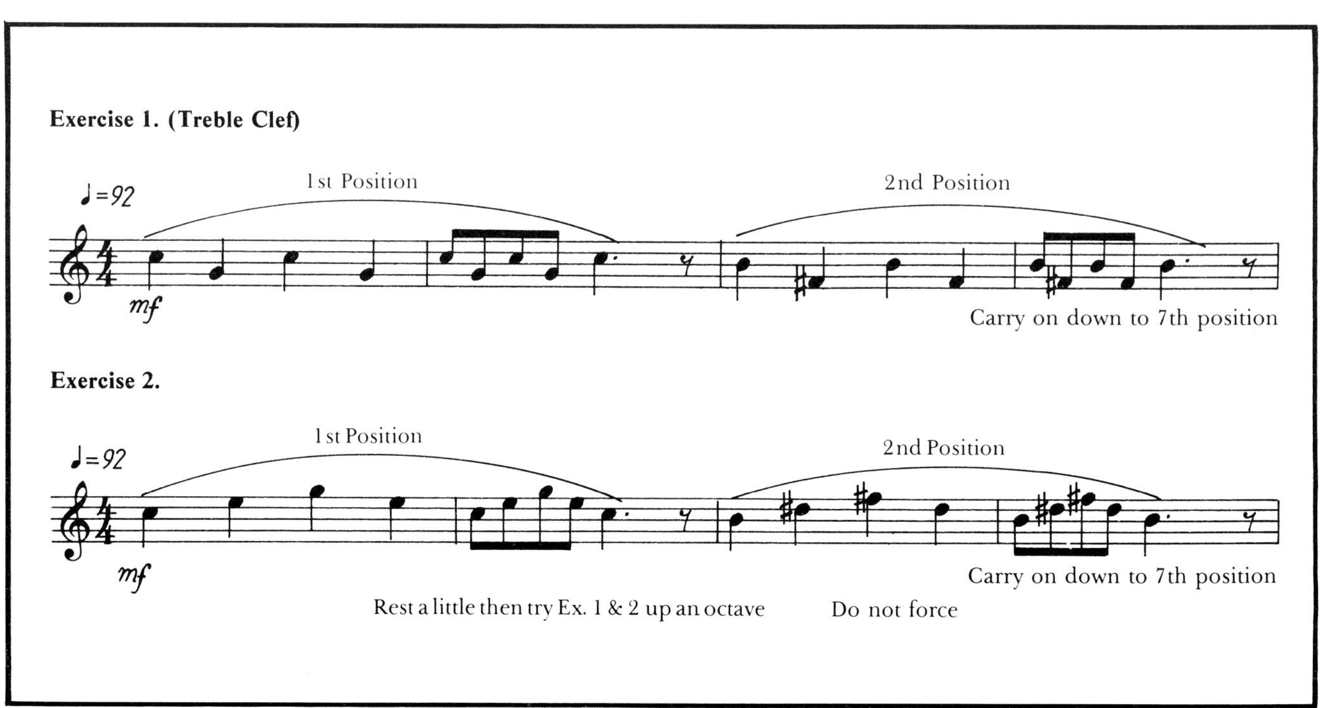

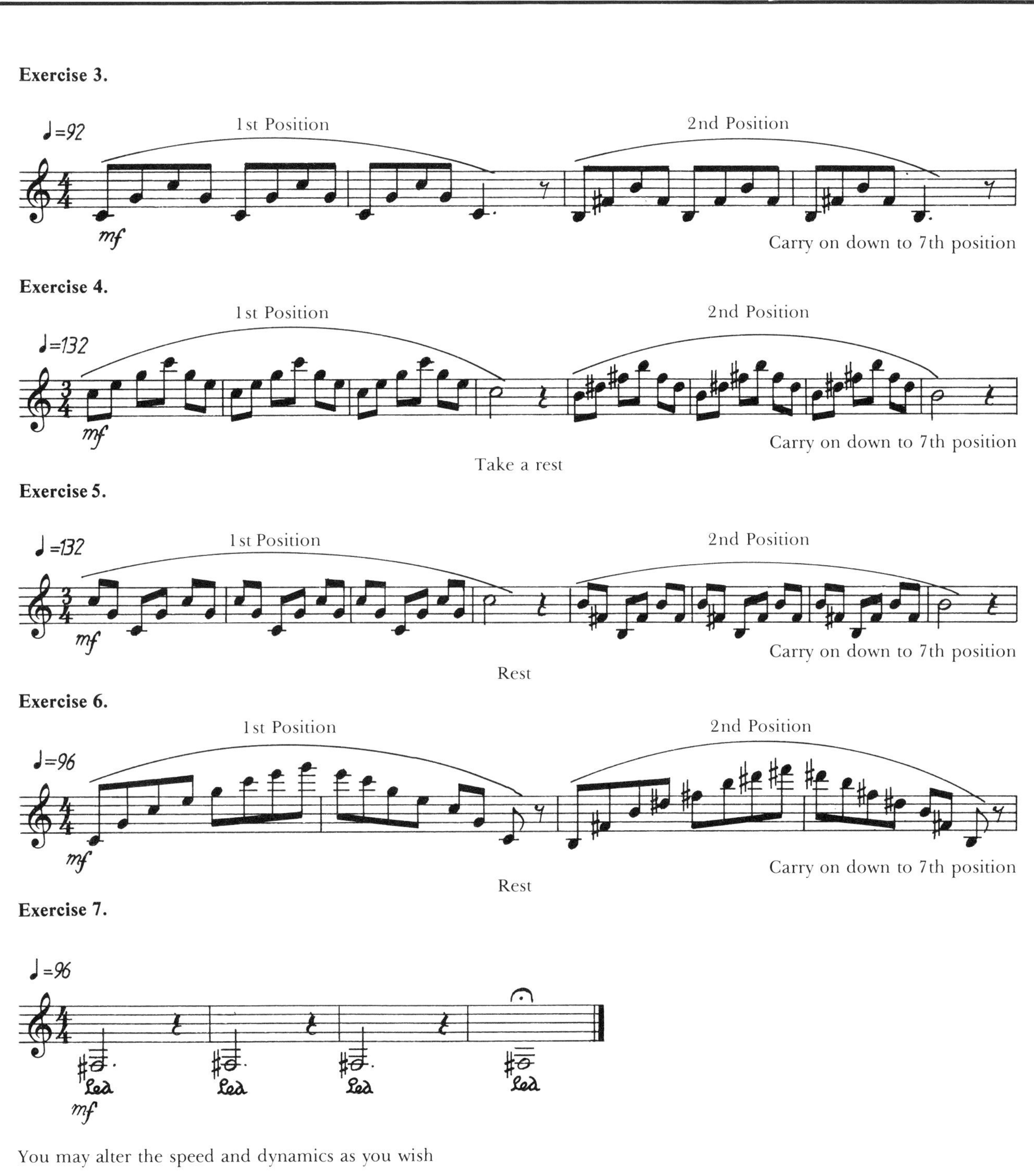
Exercise 3.
♩=92
1st Position
2nd Position
mf
Carry on down to 7th position
Exercise 4.
♩=132
1st Position
2nd Position
mf
Carry on down to 7th position
Take a rest
Exercise 5.
♩=132
1st Position
2nd Position
mf
Carry on down to 7th position
Rest
Exercise 6.
♩=96
1st Position
2nd Position
mf
Carry on down to 7th position
Rest
Exercise 7.
♩=96
mf
You may alter the speed and dynamics as you wish

Breathing

Breathing is one of the most important factors in playing a brass instrument.

Look at it this way: in the world of pop music, a keyboard player or a guitarist will first switch on his electric supply which is his source of power, after which he can play his instrument any way he wishes. Once he has that power, he's made!

Brass players have to make their own power supply. The way we do it is to inhale breath, then to exhale that breath in a controlled way.

It's no good breathing ordinarily, we have to do it in the most efficient way we can. We must use the diaphragm and fill it from the bottom, just like filling a bucket of water. Try to imagine you are going under water and take in as much breath as you can. Push your diaphragm right out at the bottom, start to fill from the bottom and gradually work your way up until you are using your chest as well. (Don't raise your shoulders.)

Now just hold it there and take stock of the situation. You now have a good supply of air — your power supply. Feel the firmness round your sides and back; use these muscles and the diaphragm as a support for your playing. No matter if it be *fff* of *ppp* you will need that support. Now how to use that supply of air: exhale through your open throat, on through the embouchure, right round the instrument, out of the bell and project on and on and on.

When you start to exhale, think of squeezing a tube of toothpaste from the bottom, gradually working your way up to the top. Your diaphragm will now go in, just the opposite from when you inhale. Plenty of good walking or running will help your breathing. You can work out your breathing in so many steps. Keep as fit as you can, it will certainly help with your breathing. I don't need to say, I'm sure, that smoking will harm it.

You will find that your air supply will go faster when you are playing in the lower register; in the upper register I find that the air stream has to be more concentrated with greater intensity.

For loud playing you will find that your power unit will give you all the air and control you require, whilst for soft and particularly high playing, good breathing and control of the air stream will make all the difference to your playing. When an electrical power supply falters or stops, so the sound will falter or stop; it is just the same with our power supply. Be conscious of it at all times.

Always take in enough air for the phrase you are about to play. On the other hand, don't take in too much; it can be very uncomfortable if you are trying to get rid of some air and play at the same time.

Try to take your intake of breath just before you play; shall we say on an up-beat. Sometimes, because of difficult phrases, you have to 'snatch' a breath.

Remember, correct breathing is *all important* to playing a brass instrument.

Scales

I realise that many students look upon scale practice as a terrible bore.

I don't think so; they can be fun to play and they will get you out of all sorts of trouble with regard to your general playing.

What I think is a good idea is to play gradually through all the scales, major, minor and chromatic. Try not only to *learn* them, but also to *memorise* them so that you are not tied to a study book.

Play them over one, two or three octaves, whatever your range will allow.

Concentrate on intonation by playing them slowly; be careful with your slide movements and listen to every note.

Play them at a regular tempo and work out your breathing. After this you can work up your speed and use various types of tonguing, *legato* and *staccato*.

Play also two quavers, four semiquavers, triplet quavers all to each beat. You can also use them for double and triple tonguing. (See chapter on tonguing. Page 83).

The wonderful thing about playing scales is that, if you do them all over the two and three octaves, you will have covered every note on the instrument.

Whenever I practise, even during my warm up if I'm pushed for time, I play a variety of scales with a variety of articulations.

By making scales part of my daily practise, I can play just as happily in one key as in another.

Intonation

I'm sure many of us have heard some one give a performance which in other respects has been almost perfect, marred only by bad intonation. It is something which grates on the human ear. Members of the listening public can tell that something is wrong with the performance and you don't have to be a musician to know. It can be either sharp or flat or just off. Musicians tend to say that it's 'sour'. It doesn't need to be the complete piece — just the odd note — and it does really spoil everything. It is essential for performers to listen to themselves all the time.

As trombone players, we have to listen in a special way. We have only the positions on the slide and our own ears to tell us whether we are in or our of tune.

I fully realise that text books will instruct us in the exact distance between the slide positions but, in my experience, I have found that each make of trombone will vary. Not only that, but each individual instrument of the same make will also vary. By all means take notice of what text books say about positions but you will have to make the final judgement by your own ear.

* * *

You can practise getting used to making the adjustments by playing a simple four note arpeggio; for example starting on middle F concert, go to A and get that interval really in tune, then on to C, get that interval right and so on to the upper F.

You can make the adjustment by either moving the slide or by tightening or slackening the embouchure. You can practise this by playing scales and melodies. Whatever you do, try it slowly at first so that you have enough time to make your adjustment for the correct intonation.

* * *

Everyone does not have 'perfect pitch' but I would say that the average musician has a pretty good ear. This natural aptitude can be improved.

A few ideas on this are:

* * *

Sing a note and then play it on the piano or on your instrument. See how you were for pitch. You will find this will improve as you go along. Incidentally, when I speak of singing you don't have to have a wonderful voice; you need only make the sound. It's a good idea to use a little singing to help with your playing; it will not only help with your pitching but also, if you have a difficult phrase to play, sing it over first. It can help tremendously.

Many of my colleagues do this. We often do it as a section when there is something difficult to phrase, in order to get it together. It's all part of music making.

Try to make yourself aware of the everyday sounds you hear all around you. See if you can get the correct pitch of a motor horn, squealing brakes and similar things. It's fun and it will help with your pitching. One other point: brass players do have to know the sound of a note before they play it, both the pitch and the quality. Listening to everyday sounds and identifying the pitch will help you with intonation.

* * *

Whilst were on the subject, here is a tip on tuning the trombone I always tune mine a little sharp. That is to say that I adjust my tuning slide so that when I play a middle B flat concert with the slide completely closed I would sound sharp to the sound from which I am taking my pitch. If I move my slide down about ½" I will be in tune on that B flat. This does mean that I have to move down a little for all seven positions. This is called 'playing down the slide'.

The reason this is often done is quite simple. On any trombone there are notes in the closed position which are quite flat. When I play any of these I am able to move the slide up a little and so I can compensate the flatness in pitch of these notes. Another reason for 'playing down the slide' is that you will be able to use a shallow vibrato in the closed position without playing flat.

* * *

Symphony players often have springs fitted at the top of the slides so they can also use this method of compensating for flat notes in the home position.

I can assure you that many well known players use this method of tuning sharp.

It is essential that you use you ears all the time to make sure that you are in tune on every note. It is a good idea to ask another player to check your tuning. I often do this.

Lip Trills

I don't know of any easy way to achieve success with regard to lip trills.

You must practise them slowly at first and gradually build up speed; the pattern for so doing is laid down in your study books.

The movement of the embouchure to make the trill possible to ascend to the above note of the trill and back again is very small; be careful not to overdo this movement.

I advise you also to cut down the pressure as much as possible.

Sometimes in big-band music, we have to play a shake. This is the same as a lip trill except that the change from note to note is at a fairly fast speed. The sound is rougher than that of a perfect lip trill; it is mostly used to create excitement from a brass section. The dynamic range can be anything from *mp* to *ff*.

A good way of strengthening the embouchure is to put in a tight mute and blow a series of lip trills at a good *ff* then take a rest.

The development of the lip trill will, of course, help your general flexibility. Concentrate on pushing the air stream through the instrument especially when playing trills and shakes.

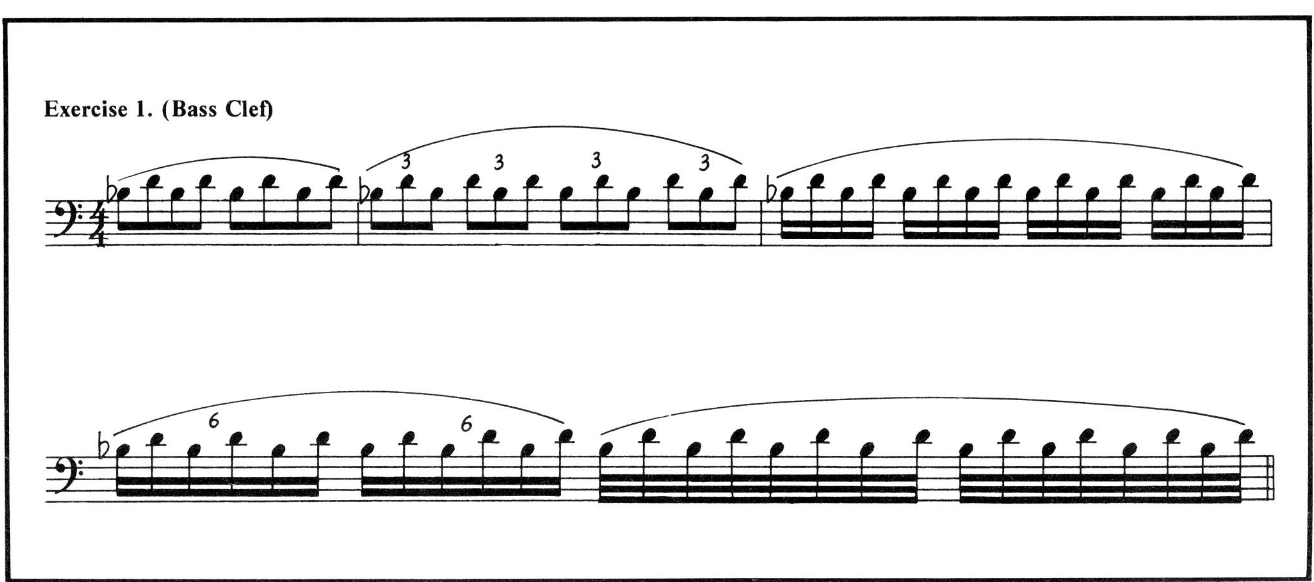

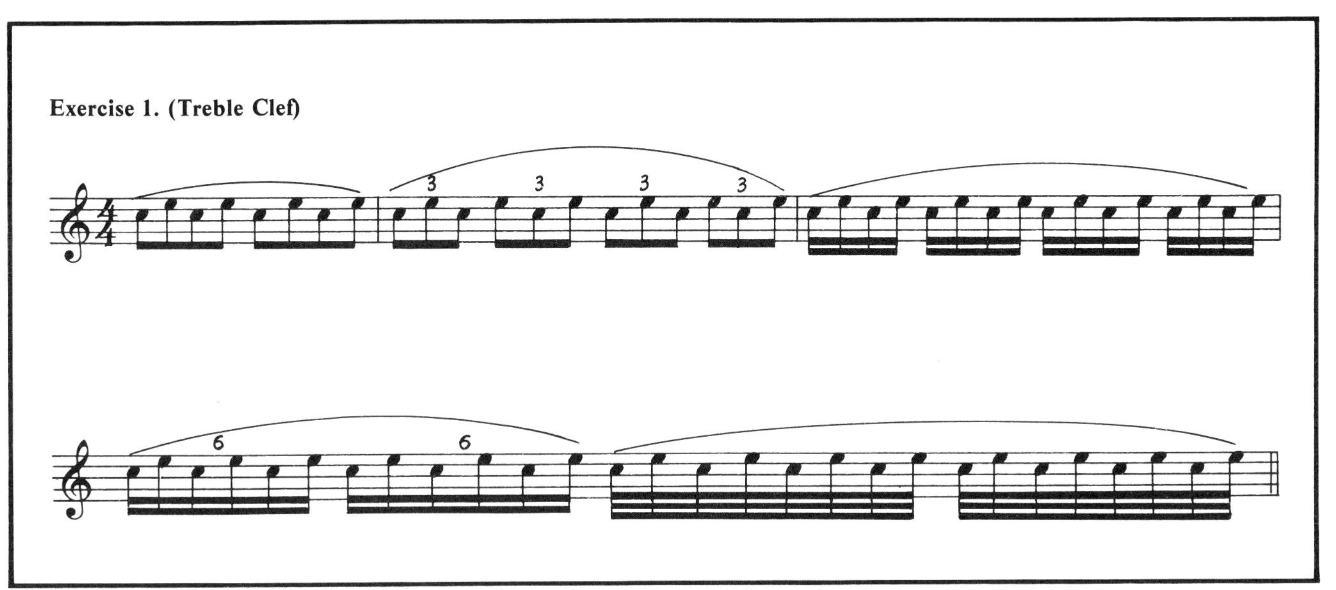
Exercise 1. (Treble Clef)
3
3
3
3
6
6

Vibrato

Let me say right away that we should all be capable of playing any note on the trombone with a completely straight sound. By that I mean with no vibrato or wobble. That is the true sound of the trombone. The vibrato is only used to enhance the sound for certain styles of playing.

1. The Slide Vibrato

This is the one which I think is best for playing tunes, melodies or anything which requires a very lyrical style. It is used with beautiful results by the world's foremost ballad players, including, of course, Tommy Dorsey.

It is a good idea to make a point of listening to these players, so that you can get the sound of their vibrato into your head. The vibrato is made by moving the slide a little above and a little below the note. Start the note cold before you add the slide movement. Your right hand and arm should not be stiff nor too loose. Aim for it to be relaxed but in control so that you can get a really nice movement with the slide.

The slide movement can be between one or two inches and the speed is purely a matter of taste. For this type of playing, I favour a medium slide movement and a medium speed.

Remember that this type of vibrato should be a thing of great beauty. *A good way to practise it is to play any note in the upper middle register and just move the slide a little above and below the note. Get used to hearing the variation in the pitch.*

Then try to make the slide movement more rhythmic. At this stage it will probably sound pretty terrible but, if you keep at it, it will gradually improve.

Now play any scale in a slow four using this vibrato, four beats on each note. You should begin to hear some improvement.

Next start playing tunes and use this vibrato. Do this a great deal until you are accustomed to this way of playing.

Listen to your intonation all the time; it is possible to play out of tune when using a slide vibrato. Avoid using the closed position because, with moving your slide for the vibrato, you are going to be very flat. You must use alternative slide positions.

Many first-class players tune the instrument quite sharp and then play everything down the slide a little. This really means, of course, that each position including the closed position will be sharp in pitch so that it is necessary to move down for everything. It is then possible to use the slide vibrato in the closed position. One very important point to note: when using this tuning sharp method, only your ear can tell whether you are in tune or not, so treat it with great caution. One other point: I don't think that the slide vibrato is suitable for playing in the lower middle register and certainly not in the bottom register. Mention will be made of this later in this chapter.

2. The Lip Vibrato

This can be used like the slide vibrato for melodic playing; also for jazz and for some legitimate playing. It works well in the lower middle and even in the bottom register of the trombone so that you can use it to take over from the slide vibrato when the melody goes into the lower register. Don't forget that the principle is the same as with the slide vibrato. The speed and depth can be adjusted according to taste.

A good idea for practising is to think of it as a lip trill which never reaches the other note.

Play a middle B flat concert. Now instead of reaching the D above and the F below go through the mechanism of doing so but never really get those other notes. You will then have a B flat slightly raised and flattened. Do this many times and then try to make your variation in pitch more rhythmic. Again, it will still sound pretty terrible; keep at it then go on to scales and melodies as you did for slide vibrato. I find that for general playing this type of vibrato should not be too deep and of a medium speed.

Practise it a great deal so as to get used to the sound and feel of playing this way. I have heard some of our leading symphony players, including Dennis Wick, use this type of vibrato when playing solo passages. The results have been marvellous.

3. The Head Vibrato

This is achieved by way of nodding the head, it can look ugly and, when it is abused, can sound horrible. On the other hand it does have its place. In blues and jazz, playing with a gentle nod of the head towards the end of the note can sound great.

Practise is on single notes, then on to scales and so on to melodies.

In general playing, guard against overdoing it; I would still prefer either the slide or the lip vibrato.

4. The Throat Vibrato

I don't recommend this for trombone playing. I like to keep my throat open; that's all I'm concerned with.

5. The Diaphragm Vibrato

Here again, I am so concerned with breathing from my diaphragm I can't use it for any other purpose.

In my general playing, I sometimes use slide, lip and head vibrato, letting one take over from the other and on occasions I will use a combination of slide and lip vibrato.

Try and remember that, with all forms of vibrato, the rule should be, *'in good taste'.* Furthermore, don't neglect your non-vibrato playing.

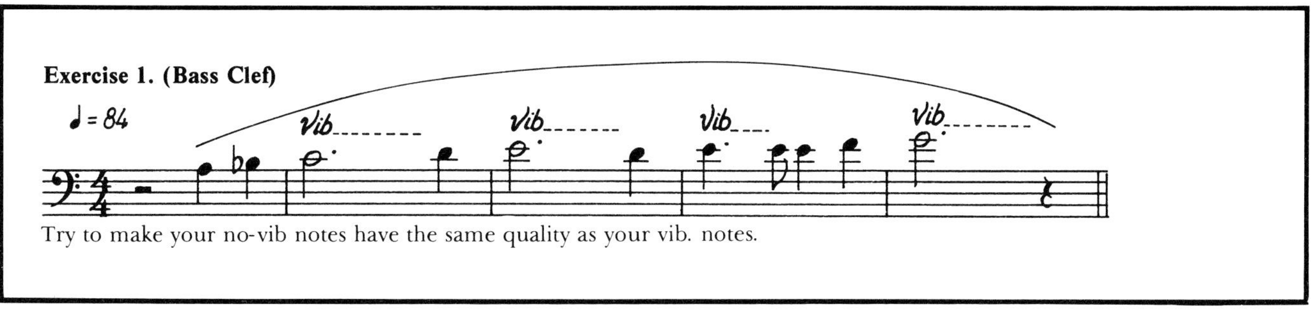

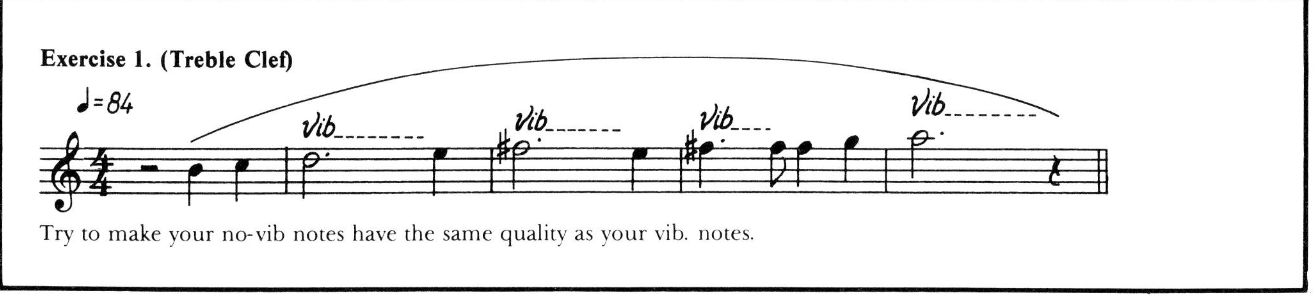

Shifting and Positions

When you look in most study books concerning the seven positions on the slide you will find certain measurements given, such as 3½″ 3$\frac{3}{16}$″ and so on. Use these only as a guide; let your ear dictate where that position actually is. Experience has taught me that, on different makes of instrument and with each individual instrument, these positions will vary slightly.

It is a good idea when you are practising sometimes to close your eyes, move to another position and listen carefully to the intonation. In the darkness it seems your hearing and pitch are much more sensitive.

Be careful with the lower positions 5, 6 and 7; it's easy to be inaccurate down there.

Remember that your slide movements should be fast but avoid jerking which can show in your playing. The use of alternative positions is a *must*, so we shall need to work on this.

Study your position chart and make sure you know where all the alternative positions are. Try to cut your slide movements to a minimum and take note of the various tones or sounds which the same note has in its various positions. They will vary, but with use, you can get to know them better.

Spend time playing a certain note in the 'home' position, then play it in the alternative positions. Take note of its sound and texture, also the intonation, and where you have to move the slide for the best results.

One case in point where you will really need the alternative positions is in the playing of various 'glisses'.

Remember when I was speaking about slide vibrato and not using the 'home' positions because of being flat, this of course is another case where you will have to use the outward positions. Here are some of the notes and positions which I use a lot. I also do some in the top register which I work out for myself as this can be a very personal thing.

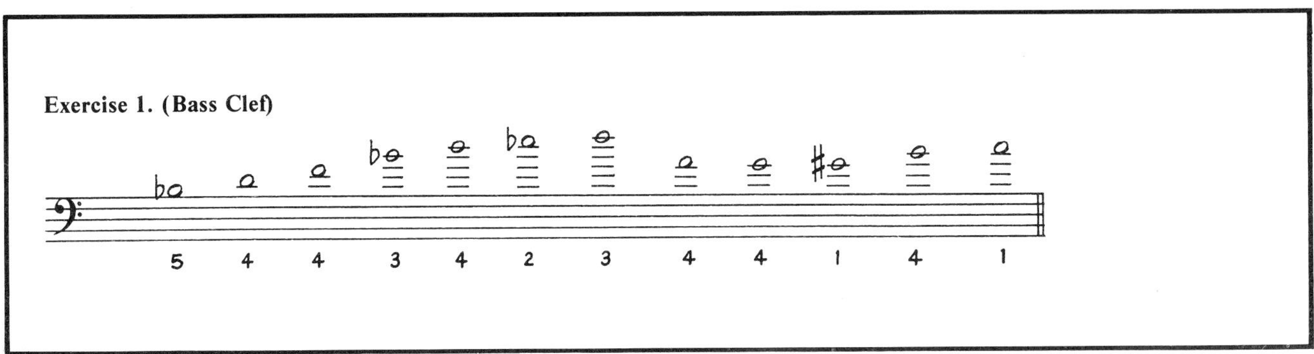

Exercise 1. (Treble Clef)

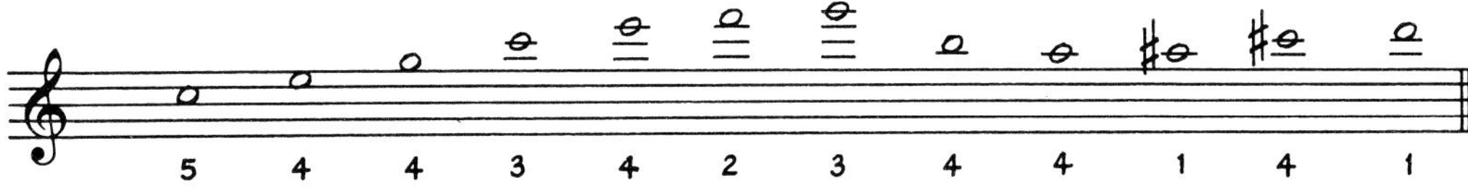

Non-pressure Playing

People often ask me 'Do you play non-pressure?' I have to say that I do not; furthermore, as far as I can recall, neither do any of my colleagues. What we do use is the *least pressure possible.*

You see, it is essential to use sufficient pressure to close the seal between the mouthpiece and the embouchure; if not, the air will escape. But be careful to cut this pressure down to a minimum.

I well remember in my early days, my father took me to see what he described as 'a rather wonderful feat in brass playing!' We were taken to a garden shed; inside stood a very good cornet player and, in front of him suspended from the roof on a piece of rope, was his cornet. With his hands behind his back he proceeded to play some exercises. Well, he certainly did make some sounds and played a great many notes, but I can assure you that the results were nothing to be proud of in the way of quality. At times, it resembled the cries of an animal being severely dealt with. However it was all very entertaining.

I try to make a point of making myself conscious of pulling the mouthpiece away from my embouchure. Only very slightly of course; this will help to ensure that I am not using too much pressure. *You can practise doing this sort of thing. Play any scale of one octave in the middle register. Play it softly, pull the mouthpiece away from the embouchure slightly and see how you get on.*

Repeat this many times going gradually into the upper and lower registers. You will find after a time you are using less pressure.

I find that in the middle range playing up to *mf* I can get away with using hardly any pressure at all; on the other hand, in the top or bottom registers especially playing loudly, I do certainly use a fair amount of pressure.

I'm sure we have all seen from time to time players really pressing and struggling to make those top notes, their lips battered almost to a pulp. No one ever made it that way. I will go into the subject of 'high notes' later; in the meantime, 'non pressure'? I don't think so. But for sure, *'the least pressure possible!'*

Pedal Notes

When played softly these can sound beautiful; when played loud they can be frightening. They do have their place but, other than that, I have found them very good for strengthening the embouchure.

They are the foundation of our range and we have to remember one or two important points. The embouchure and mouthpiece positions should not change when playing them. Think of the same sort of shape as when you whistle; corners of the mouth turned down. You will need a good strong air column. Do your practice starting above the pedal range and work down into it; then you can take notice of your embouchure position. Vary the dynamics, do some at — *mf* — *pp* — *ff.*

False Tones

On an ordinary tenor trombone — that is a trombone without a B flat and F attachment or trigger as musicians sometimes call them — there is a gap in between the low E concert and the pedal series starting on pedal B flat. In actual fact, the so-called gap of five notes — E flat, D, D flat, C and B natural can be played.

This is the way to do it:

Play the low E in the seventh position as normal; have in your mind the pitch of the next note down — E flat. Take a good breath, relax the embouchure, move the slide down from the normal third position to the fourth, play the note and be sure to push the sound through. It takes a great deal of air.

Follow the same procedure with the D, instead of fourth position get it in the Fifth. Do the same with D flat and C.

With the low B natural you will find that you have nearly run out of slide; you can still get the note if you go right out to the bottom of the slide.

Now play the pedal B flat in the closed position. Don't be put off if your early efforts are not very good; keep at it. The sound can be as bad as blowing into a gas pipe, the more you do it the better it will get.

Remember, you need a good breath, relaxed embouchure, down one position and follow through. Have the pitch of the note in your mind before you play it; it may help if you play the note up an octave first.

These notes are not for general performance, they can be used as a show off in solo playing. I am guilty of this myself!

Their best use is in practice. I find that they do relax the embouchure and use them sometimes if my embouchure is feeling tired.

Players, with a trigger can still use this form of practice by not using the trigger and following the same procedure.

Exercise 2. (Bass Clef)

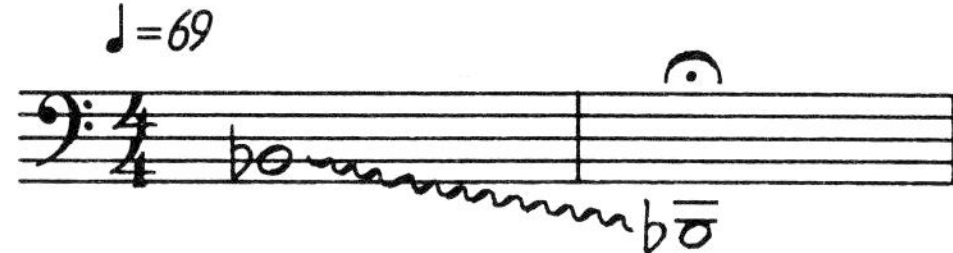

Slowly try to slur down to the pedal

Play this pattern down to Low E

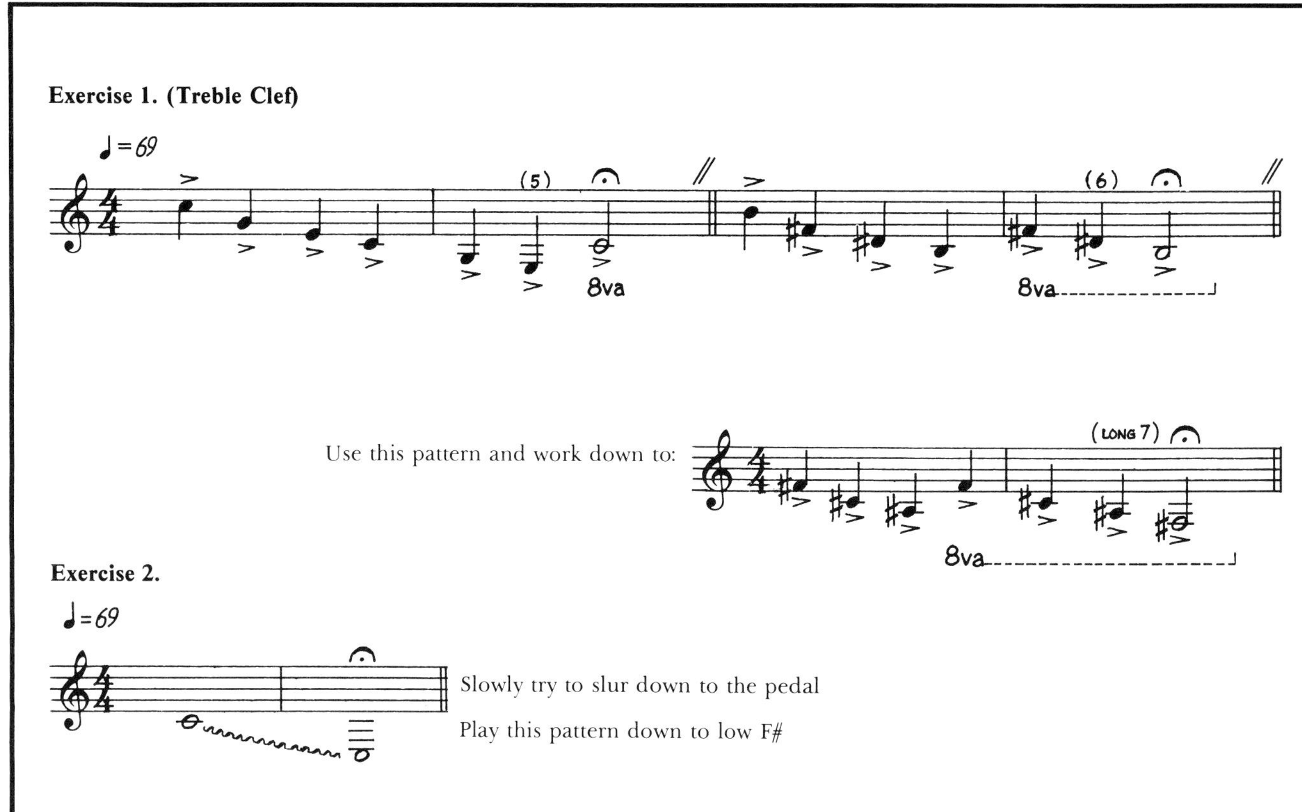

Section Playing

The first thing we need is pride in the section, the ability to get on well together even if you are all different types. You must be able to talk about things to get the best results.

The responsibility for making decisions will, of course, fall on the leader or principal. Here is a point for your principal: always try to make the rest of the section feel important, because they *are*. Balance is a prime factor; never overblow the next guy. Furthermore, if you can't hear him comfortably the guess is that you are playing too loud.

Another strong point is intonating. Listen to your note in the chord and, if necessary, adjust the pitch. Bass trombonists have a great responsibility because frequently they are playing the root of the chord and, if that is out, everything else will be wrong.

A good idea is to play some sustained chords slowly with no vibrato — just listen for the balance and intonation . . .

When you are playing these, don't use a vibrato; just a nice straight-through sound. You can use just a little vibrato for effect sometimes. Another point regarding the use of vibrato in the middle and lower part any sort of vibrato can sound silly. I have found that sometimes it works better if the lead plays with vibrato and the others play without. If you do this, try to warm the sound a little so that it doesn't sound too hard.

Regarding rhythmic playing, be careful not to drag. It's easy for a bass trombone player to get behind because he has some tough things to play. You should all make yourselves very aware of 'time' in all types of music. Remember, no matter if there are two or five of you, you are a section, so work at it.

We can all listen to the finest sections in the world playing all types of music, surely some of the most musical sounds around.

Playing Jazz Trombone

Jazz music should contain emotion and should swing. It should have an effect on the performer and on the listener.

It can be simplicity itself or be extremely involved. Jazz music has been going on in various ways for many years; some of to-day's jazz had reached a very advanced standard. I have no idea which way it will go in the future but, be sure, it will find a way and it will go on as it always has.

Now you don't have to like this or that; in the same way you don't have to play this way or that way. Think about it and listen all you can. You will, or course, be influenced but eventually try and play the way you want to and like the things you want to. Though you are a trombone player you must listen to and learn from all jazz players regardless of the instrument they play.

Learn about harmony, chords and chord symbols. You can get this information from books and from keyboards. Play a little on a keyboard if you can. Better still try and get some lessons from a jazz keyboard player. He or she will show you not only how to play but also about chord progressions or 'changes'.

On the trombone itself, you will need to learn and to play all the scales. Whilst doing this you can improve your tonguing, legato, fast single and doodle tonguing, all of which are very useful when playing jazz.

Learn all the chords and play arpeggios on them. Here again, do some tonguing and some lip slurring between the various intervals.

Use as many alternative positions as possible; this will help you to get around your trombone in the easiest possible way. Dispense, with the slide as much as possible. Try and practise with a metronome to help with your time.

Vary your dynamics quite a lot, sometimes loud, sometimes a whisper. Whatever you do, play with feeling no matter if it be a melody or a mass of notes.

There are many great jazz trombone players to listen to, but if you use as a basis Jack Teagarden, Urbie Green, J. J. Johnson, Kai Winding, Bill Watrous and our own George Chisholm and Roy Williams, it will give you a very good grounding for jazz playing.

If you are interested in jazz have a go! Take any simple melody and mess it around your own way — it's only like a theme and variations you know.

Choice of Trombones and Mouthpieces

We could talk about this subject endlessly, such a lot depends on what type of playing you are doing. Cost, also, has to be taken into consideration. Again, will the instrument be new or secondhand? I don't want to lay down a great many hard-and-fast rules but I would like to give some guidance.

If you are a good, experienced player and can afford the most expensive models, just search around until you find the one you like best. You should have a great deal of fun, although with such a wide choice available it can drive you mad!

On the other hand, if your financial resources are limited and you don't have much experience then you will need some help. Try and get some advice from your teacher or ask a well-known player. Go to a good dealer, who will also be able to advise and help.

It is often a better idea to buy a good second-hand instrument than to buy a new cheap one. Trombones have quite a long life-span and some players tend to change their instruments many times, rather like people do with cars. Other players will probably know if there's a good secondhand buy going. Ask around.

Now I'm going to deal with bass trombones. First, there are some wonderful pieces of plumbing on the market these days and according to my friends, who play bass trombones, all the well-known makes are very good. It will come down to a matter of personal preference. It is essential to have a trigger mechanism which you like, likewise the sound the feel of the 'blow'. How does it handle and will it blend with the rest of your section?

The most popular makes for bass trombones seem to be:

HOLTON BACH CONN BOOSEY & HAWKES YAMAHA KING

As for tenor trombones, it is important to have the size which is right for the type of playing you are doing. If you are playing legitimate symphonic music you must have the large bore symphonic model. This will give you the large dark sound, the ability to play very loud and very soft without any deterioration in sound. If you are playing first trombone you shouldn't have to have a trigger; if you are on second trombone you will need one.

Here again the best makes are all very good, so it will be a case of personal preference. Bear in mind that some orchestras will expect you all to play a certain make of instrument.

Some suggestions for symphony tenor trombones are as follows:

Bach 42 or 42B King 4B Conn 8H or 88H Boosey and Hawkes 547
Holton 150 or 155 Yamaha YSL 641 Selmer-Largo

A word concerning alto trombones which I really do think are a matter of personal preference. It is a difficult instrument from any angle and with special problems of intonation. I feel that the choice must be left to the player.

Studio, jazz, rock and big band players will have a wide choice,
King 2B and 3B Conn 5H and 6H also the Constellation Bach 12 and 16M
Selmer Large Holton Artist Yamaha YSL 651 Martin 'Urbie Green' model
. . . not forgetting, of course, the Boosey and Hawkes Sovereign 937 model, which I myself use and find delightful as a general-purpose trombone. All of these instruments are very fine indeed, so it's up to you.

Some models you can obtain with a trigger attachment but unless you really need one, don't bother with them. One other point, for this type of playing don't use a larger bore size; it is the wrong sound. Just remember that the world's greatest jazz and ballad soloists use or have used these models.

That leaves us with brass bands, wind bands, light orchestras and chamber groups. My advice would be to leave the bass trombones as I have already advised. For second trombones, you will have the choice between tenor trombones of the symphony world, probably with a trigger, or the studio/jazz models, again with a trigger. For first trombonists, I would advise the same instruments as for studio/big-band models with no trigger. Don't forget that you are expected to be a soloist as well as a section leader. These types of instruments would work well for this double role.

Please don't choose an instrument that is too large; remember that each trombone is one of a family and if you all play large instruments you will destroy the character of sound. One other point; you will find that all of the well known makes do a full range of student models. These are much less costly but don't forget what I said about secondhand instruments.

Now to the question of what mouthpiece to use. If you are not an experienced player do try and get some advice from a teacher or a well-known player. The choice of mouthpiece is a very individual thing because of variation in mouth and teeth formation. Let me give you a few guidelines. Never fall for any propaganda which assures you that a certain mouthpiece will make playing the trombone easy. It won't. However, the right one will help.

Have a rim which feels comfortable to your lips, not too thick though; don't forget that the mouthpiece is the go-between for you and the instrument. Make sure that the diameter is not too small or too large. The depth of cup will alter the sound so go for a medium cup. See that the hole at the bottom of the cup is not too small. If it is, it could restrict the air passage.

The shank should fit well into the mouthpipe; if it sticks out too much you could have some badly flat notes. When trying a new mouthpiece, pay attention to:

1. Comfort of rim,
2. Quality of sound,
3. Clean air passage thoughout the full range,
4. Good intonation.

Some dealers will allow you to take a mouthpiece home with you to try over a weekend. See if your dealer will allow you to do this as it's the best way to try it. When you have found the best one for you, work at it and stick with it. Don't think of changing every time something goes wrong with your playing.

Like trombones, most of the mouthpieces made by the best firms are very good.

Here is a list of mouthpieces which I know are used by some of the best players in the world:

Bass Trombones
Bach 2 G
Denis Wick 2AL

Symphony Tenor Trombones
Bach 5G
Denis Wick 5AL

Alto Trombones
Bach 11C
Denis Wick 10CS

Studio, jazz, rock, big bands and soloists
Bach 12C 11C
Denis Wick 10CS 12BS

Brass bands, wind bands, light orchestras and chamber groups
Bach 12C 11C 7C
Denis Wick 10CS 12BS

I use a Denis Wick 10CS or a Bach 11C for my Sovereign 937 Boosey and Hawkes trombone, and a Denis Wick 5AL for my Boosey & Hawkes symphony model and on my Sovereign euphonium.

Nerves

I really don't know of anyone who doesn't suffer with nerves at some time or another. It can vary in intensity and in regularity.

The most important thing is to deal with it in the best way possible. Individuals have different ways of sorting out their own nerves.

The great danger for anyone is the use of artificial aids, be they drink, tablets or the syringe. They all slow down the mental powers and can become very much a habit. After a couple of drinks, everything seems much better and you even think that you're playing better. The point is that only *you* think this! As time goes by, you will need more and more to reach the desired effect and eventually end up in a fearful condition. Let me say here and now that I am not preaching against drink. As a fun thing it is great; I've had many laughs with fellow musicians over a drink after a concert. Likewise I do respect Salvation Army Bandsmen for their principle of being teetotal; we have also had many a laugh together over nothing more than a cup of tea.

I do feel strongly about using any kind of artificial relaxant because I've had the experience of having some of my close friends, who have been great players and very nice people, eventually fall by the wayside both professionally and in their private lives though excessive use of drink and other stimulants. Some so badly abused their bodies that they died from the result of drink problems. What a waste of talent!

Now what to try to do about nerves.

Make sure that whatever you have to play, you can do it with confidence; in other words, do your homework and preparation — don't leave anything to chance.

Try to relax as much as possible. My old boss Ted Heath told me to slow down all my movements, including my breathing, when it became time to go out front to play a solo.

Another point; most of us enjoy making music so try to enjoy your playing and make the most of it.

Concentration is also very important. It's very easy to be distracted so keep your mind on what you're doing.

Now, if you didn't play well on one particular occasion — maybe you missed a few notes — don't go home and give your wife or mother a bad time. Don't kick the cat or go into a big sulk or be off-hand with your mates. Think about what went wrong, try to put it right for next time and then forget about it. Your playing is very important to you but there are many more important things in life itself.

Remember, nerves are all part of being a performer. Therefore we have to live with them and control them in the best way possible.

People often say to me 'Do you ever get nervous?' They always seem surprised when I say 'Yes, I do.' You see the greater one's reputation the more the public expects of you. It's easy for an audience to hear me play not very well sometimes and to go away and say such things as 'Yes, I heard Don Lusher; he didn't play well, he's going off you know.'

Well, I hope it's not true, but it's very important to me. Don't forget that, besides making music, it is my livelihood so, like all of you, I do the best I can to control my nerves.

Care of the Instrument

This is something which is either taken for granted or can be overlooked. I can well remember the times when someone has said 'Have a blow on my instrument'. After taking a breath I have nearly retched as the stink and taste of old beer and curry hit me. Likewise, I have seen instrument cases so dirty that I would not like to put a hand inside.

Now I know its not as bad as this generally, but here are some points which I keep an eye on.

Wash through the trombone and mouthpiece once a week. I use a soapy water and then rinse it out with clean warm water using a brush or rod.

For my slide I use a little cream, rubbed on the inner slide, spread evenly over the stockings and then over the rest of the slide. Spray water on and then work the slide well over it. I find that oil doesn't work for me and I hate the smell.

On a new slide you will have to do this a lot. I usually clean the inside of the outer slide with a silver polish by means of a rod, then the inner slide just to wear it in a little.

If you are not going to use the trombone for some time, dry off the slide.

The outside of the instrument should be kept clean and bright; a set of brass instruments can be quite a glamorous sight, you know.

Be careful to put your instrument in a safe place whenever you can. If I do have any damage I get it repaired right away, especially damage concerning the slide. It will hamper your playing and give an uncomfortable feeling. Look after the rotary valves if you have them. Don't neglect the case.

I once had a pupil who complained about the way his trombone 'wasn't playing'. I cleaned it for him and pulled out from the slide a piece of sludge six inches long!

Look after your trombone; it can be a great friend. Don't — and it can be an enemy.

To we trombone players, slides are very precious pieces of equipment. Even among the best of instruments some slides are better than others. We clean them and work out the best lubricants to put on them. How much to put on and how often? It's all a lifetimes' study.

Above all we really do try to avoid getting the slide dented. Even a slight knock can have a bad effect. Exactly the same thing happens when pressure is put on the slide; we then have what is called a strain. Either a strain or a dent can make the life of a trombone player sheer hell. We try, therefore, to avoid getting a knock or, worse still, dropping the trombone.

One of my friends — trombonist and arranger, Bill Geldard — was playing one night at Green's Playhouse, Glasgow with Johnny Dankworth's Band; he was enjoying the music and really into his playing. In a difficult passage he shot to the seventh position and, quick as a flash, it happened! The slide left his hand, fell over the edge of the bandstand and on to the dance floor — a very good dance floor at that, as slippery as they come. On and on it went like a torpedo, missing the dancers by inches until it passed out of sight. Eventually, some kind dancer picked it up and returned it to Bill; all eyes were on him as he prepared to put the slide back together. With a pale face and a trembling hand he placed the escapee into its rightful position. He pulled it on, everyone waited for the verdict with bated breath.

Bill's face broke into a watery smile, colour returned to his cheeks as he said, 'Well, it seems better than ever!'

THIS TREATMENT IS NOT TO BE RECOMMENDED!

General Hints

Never overblow. A true *ff* is a wonderful sound to hear from a brass section. If you try to go past this point, the sound will only become nasty and thin.

Always have some sound in reserve. Not only will it sound bad but you can do short-term damage to the embouchure. If you make a habit of it you will damage the embouchure for a long time.

When playing in an ensemble, remember that you are only a part of what is going on. Listen to the internal balance; if you can't hear the instrument next to you, you are most likely playing too loudly. Listen for intonation. I try to take my relative pitch from the bass line. Make sure that the phrasing is together; you may need to talk about this at rehearsal. Keep an eye on your music and one eye on the conductor. Follow his indications all the way, even when you don't fully agree with them.

Try to take an interest in all types of music; the world of music is so large. Don't be narrow in your outlook.

Listen to and watch good players, especially if you have the opportunity to see and hear the best in the world. We can learn so much from them.

Don't forget to blow the water out of your instrument just before you play, using the water key, of course. Water can build up quicker than you think.

Take frequent rests when doing your practice. I think it's a good idea to stand during practice.

Try and allow sufficient time to arrive early for a rehearsal or concert; you need time to unpack and make yourself comfortable, time to have a warm up and maybe a look at the music. The same applies when you are going for a lesson.

Learn as much as you can about the theory of music. Know the musical terms and signs. Spend a little time whenever you can playing in clefs which you don't normally use. At some time or another you could have to use the bass, tenor, alto, treble clef concert and treble clef B flat as used in brass bands.

It's a good idea to practice transposition; trombone players sometimes have to play from horn parts.

People often ask me if I take my trombone on holiday with me; these days I have to say 'yes'! Not that I wish to become a slave to it but it's quite possible to jump right in at the deep end after a break, so you've got to be in reasonable shape. It's no use telling the people you're working for, or an audience for that matter, that you haven't played for so many days. They are not interested. They are paying money and they expect, and indeed are entitled to, a good performance.

In the days when I was with a regular band like Ted Heath, the band would break and everyone would go on holiday. It was good then to leave the instrument alone. I used to take a mouthpiece with me and do some buzzing. Then, after returning home in the remaining days before we started work with the band, I would really get down to a good general practice. I found that, with a regular playing band, I could soon get back into form.

As a freelance studio musician and soloist, it's not as easy because I don't get such a consistent blow.

I go away on holiday for a week, or maybe two. For the first part I try not to even think about the trombone, let alone play it. But for the last few days I do some buzzing and some playing. I start off gently and gradually build it up, sometimes muted and sometimes open. I try to look upon it as a pleasure and not as a chore.

If I'm going home to a concert date within a few days, then, of course, I have to work a little harder at it. It's not always possible to plan these things, you know, but I try not to leave anything to chance.

Aim to keep yourself as fit as possible — do some daily exercise and play some sport. When you feel well in yourself you seem to be able to play that much better.

No matter at what standard of playing we are, we should all be sure to give of our best at all times.

Have the best teacher you can afford; don't become discouraged when you don't seem to be making much progress.

Remember that it's very easy to criticise someones performance, try and be constructive with it.

Think of your own playing from all angles.

Well at least you have reached the end. I do hope that you have found it all beneficial and enjoyable.

Keep the book handy so that you can use it for reference.

With best wishes

Sincerely,

Don Lusher.